ABOUT THE AUTHOR

Marlène is a life lover before anything else, and a chef.

France is her place of birth but she likes to call herself 'a citizen of the world'. Her greediness to learn about different culture brought her to travel around the world with her backpack.

After living in England and in the US working in restaurants, as a food stylist and food writer, she is now an established chef, cooking for events, giving cooking classes and has just opened a restaurant in her city, Nice.

MARLÈNE DULERY

My French Secrets

How Food Lovers Stay Slim

AUSTIN MACAULEY PUBLISHERS™

LONDON • CAMBRIDGE • NEW YORK • SHARJAH

A CIP catalogue record for this title is available from the British Library.

ISBN 9781035806768 (Paperback)
ISBN 9781035806775 (ePub e-book)

www.austinmacauley.com

First Published 2024
Austin Macauley Publishers Ltd®
1 Canada Square
Canary Wharf
London
E14 5AA

DEDICATION

To my dad, who passed away when this book was still in process,
who taught me to love and respect food. I can still see him whistling
in front of the stove while preparing us a lunch made for the kings.

To my mum, who had always believed in me
even through my awkward moments.

I love you both, so much.

ACKNOWLEDGEMENTS

A huge hug to Anne-Lyse. Without her, the writing of this
book wouldn't even have begun. She has been (and still is) a
friend, an encouragement and a photographer when needed
(in that special case it was in my kitchen in San Francisco).

Thank you to my friend Alyssa in Chicago – author, CEO,
wine lover and so much more, who always gives me precious
advice – and her friend Sophie in New York City, who
explained the process of writing and editing a book to me.

Thank you to Valérie Casado, artist, who lent me her
wonderful plates and dishes without knowing me at all.

Thank you to Natacha, naturopath who contributed to this book,
to Anna Jarota, agent in Paris. And thank you to Stéphanie, my
friend from back in the old days in London, who also made a
big contribution to this book with her wine expert's eyes.

CONTENTS

A NOTE FROM THE AUTHOR

B EING FRENCH is an art form, and we French are justifiably proud of our Gallic identity.

We are known for many things, mainly for our culture and elegance but also for being a little rude! However, one thing which always comes up in conversations when we talk about France is our *joie-de-vivre*, our capacity to enjoy life with all its pleasures, our well-being. We are also known for eating everything while staying slim and healthy.

I didn't notice until I lived abroad that my way of eating and living could be an example, could be shared and could benefit people looking for the path to a better lifestyle. So I started to observe my habits, gather memories from my childhood, ask my friends about their lives and their habits and take notes. This book project started then, when I was living in the US and the UK, when I was travelling around, when I was a French woman living abroad.

There are many things I do naturally, as I grew up that way. My mum was raised this way too, my grandmother and so on; our lifestyle is a collection of good habits, of things we do without even thinking about it. These things are our secrets passed on within French families for generations. I guess that eating what we want and staying slim and healthy is the result of knowing these secrets.

When I worked as a cooking instructor at X restaurants, many people asked me how I could be a chef and stay slim. When the same question kept coming up again and again, I thought that I should pass on my French secrets to all the people who wish for better. I decided to address it in this book. I see it as a little bible of good habits, of rules to follow for lifestyle, healthy eating and well-being, a way into enjoying life as we do in France, a book that everybody could carry when in need of inspiration for a last-minute dinner with friends, ideas for a weekly menu, for a nice meal à deux or a delicious lunch just for yourself and for learning how to feel good whilst indulging in all these pleasures.

I will guide you through your daily routine, your organisation in the kitchen and pantry and even your shopping list. I will give you 12 rules to follow to find a good balance in your life, to lose and maintain your ideal weight, to stay slim and healthy without forgetting to eat great food and be happy.

Being a chef or simply loving food doesn't mean eating all the time. I eat the food that I've known since my childhood: natural, homemade and seasonal – the food that makes me happy. If I'm totally honest, to me, being happy means having some great homemade food, good wine and staying healthy and slim. Cooking can be part of life's great pleasures – creative, sensual, satisfactory – and if you know a few basics, you can plan ahead and get organised. It is not difficult! Everybody can do it and find pleasure in it! If, thanks to this book, some people can find their own joy and well-being, I would be the happiest woman on the planet.

But before I reveal my secrets, which may change your life for the better forever, just a few words about who I am. I was born, a bit accidentally, in the Paris region and came to Nice (where my mum is from) at six months of age. Where I was born, there is La Marne, a river passing close to where we lived with my parents and, on 'les bords de Marne' are *ginguettes,* those popular outdoor cabarets where we can eat and drink while dancing *'la Java'.* It's a beautiful and joyful place. As long as there is food and wine, I know it's a place for me; eating and drinking always make me happy. So Nice, on the Mediterranean coast, is my city. It's where I grew up, where I learnt to swim on the *Promenade des Anglais,* where I went to school, where I had my first date, my first job, where I cooked my first omelette... my first everything.

Nice is in my head and my heart when I travel and when I live abroad. I carry its taste and smell, and I miss the atmosphere. Two hundred years ago, Nice was Italian, and it still has the Latin attitude: time goes slowly, cicadas sing and any opportunity is good to have a glass of wine. There's always been this rivalry (or let's say teasing) between the north and the south of France... For football first, the PSG (Paris Saint Germain) supporters don't mix with OM (Olympic Marseille) partisans. People from the north and south don't have the same accent, the same weather... but everywhere we share the same attitude towards food and life's little pleasures.

Paris, the most romantic city in the world, is known everywhere for the *Tour Eiffel,* the most-visited monument on the planet that everybody wants to see at least once in their life... Well, that's a lot. Being French is a lot to carry, but being Parisian is even heavier, with all the latest fashion trends to follow and political philosophising to be engaging with. In the south of France, we are lucky enough to have it all. We have the sun, the sea, the mountains, the olive oil, the Niçoise salad and the rosé wine.

MY FRENCH SECRETS

We are more... let's say, simple... Our favourite sport is to sit down in the cafés' terraces, have an espresso and watch people passing by. We are slow, happy and jolly but depressed as soon as it rains for two days in a row. The *Niçois* go to the beach all year long, as swimming in cold water is healthy and good for our mood. Wrinkles are part of the living process, and we prefer growing old tanned and happy than white, unruffled and sad.

We celebrate a lot, drink rosé wine and organise picnics whenever we can. Planning a meal is part of our lives and I can tell you it is a delight! As we say, we work to live when in many other countries, people live to work. 'Just pleasure' is our motto. When you live in the south of France, you cannot be stressed; it's a stress-free region. Having a good life is our first goal. Like all Latin people, we are late to dinner parties but are always the last to leave. (After a few glasses of wine, we forget about the *chic à la Française*.) We really enjoy our food and don't think twice about ordering a glass of wine for lunch. In France, life doesn't wait.

When I was 32, after a breakup, I decided to make one of my dreams a reality: live abroad and learn English. Breakups can be inspiring! So I packed my huge suitcase and I arrived in London without knowing anyone, without a job and with no English at all.

I immediately fell in love with London and I ended up staying for nine years. London is actually my longest love story, as I am still, to this day, in love with her. After a few jobs that paid my bills, my English got better and I started to reflect on my professional life. I was in a country and city that I adored. This was already a lot, but I did this 'n' that without really having found what I loved doing. Simply making ends meet wasn't enough! So one day, I sat down and I asked myself what I really loved doing, where I felt most invigorated and most myself. All these happy moments I spent with my mum in the kitchen came to mind, all the meals I cooked for my friends and the light in their eyes when they would thank me for the happy moments we spent together at my table, all these new recipes I tried and created in my kitchen. All of a sudden, I knew that being a chef would be the best profession for me and the best job on the planet. This is what I said to myself and I set out to become one!

It turned out that combining my passion for food and my free spirit was an obvious choice. I wanted to work for myself and be free from any boss while doing what I'd always done well: cooking. I started a catering business. It's been a long process with ups and downs (actually more downs than ups at the beginning), learning the language, writing a food blog, sending newsletters to potential clients, working for free for organisations and organising cocktail parties in search of potential clients. Beginnings are never easy, but hey, I was in my element. I didn't count my hours and was working away towards a brighter future. And one day, as it sometimes happens, a bit of luck knocked at my door; a restaurant owner that I knew from one of my jobs was opening another business and wanted me on board. I knew he was going to ask me to be a receptionist again, so I told him that I would work with him only if he would give me a position in the kitchen. A bit cheeky, but I was full of goodwill and motivation. He set up a meeting with the future head chef for a food tasting and I got a job in his new restaurant.

The restaurant was Mexican and it was bliss, a great opportunity to learn so many things in such a short amount of time, new recipes, new flavours and perfumes which add variety to my cuisines to this day. Before the grand opening, we had the immense chance to be trained by Eduardo, the chef of a few restaurants in Mexico City. Eduardo is a food encyclopaedia and apart from my appetite for learning from him and also from Illie, the woman head chef, and the rest of the staff, I loved being in this kitchen. I loved doing the opening early in the morning, still tired from our double shift the past few days but happy to be the first and only one for two hours, taking time to make my *mise en place* while drinking green tea before everybody arrived.

It's also been a big life lesson. Being a woman in a kitchen full of men (most of them younger but with more experience than I had then) wasn't easy but very formative. Juggling between my job at the restaurant and my catering business development paid off eventually. I ended up having Goldman Sachs, Eventbrite and many others as my clients. I also worked in Italian and Caribbean restaurants and learnt and loved to learn about those different cuisines, different ways of working vegetables, meat or fish, finding inspiration for my recipes. Still the same heat in the kitchen, still the same double shifts almost every day... But yes, I really loved it. The decision I took back then in London when I was 32, to become a chef, was the best I ever took in my life.

Nine years later, I had a job opportunity in San Francisco. I flew to California for a two-week job and again ended up staying for longer than expected – three years this time. I told you that I am a free spirit! Beginnings were long and emotionally gruelling, but yet again, I created a new catering business, different clients, cooking classes, a YouTube channel and this book project. I wouldn't be here today, writing this book, if

I hadn't gone through this life route, through all my ups and downs. And… I can tell you now that being a rude free spirit helps!

In total, then, I lived abroad for 12 years. This is where I learnt that as French people we are seen as cultivated, elegant, as *bons vivants* but also sometimes as arrogant. At first, I didn't understand, but talking to others and observing myself helped me to reach a good distance, crucial to understanding who we are. You guessed; it turned out that I too was arrogant in my life… A fault confessed is half redressed. And just as with many other things we do without realising their deeper meaning, I surprised myself being arrogant.

All right… just one quick story. While living in San Francisco and without a penny to survive, I took a job in a restaurant, not in the kitchen but as a waitress to help ends meet, and I remember explaining to a nice lady who ordered a simple, cheap, bubbly wine that she called champagne, why champagne is champagne and why a bubbly wine cannot be called champagne. When this poor lady just wanted to get her drink to go with her eggs Benedict, she got a full explanation from the arrogant French waitress who gives lessons even when not asked! That is just one little story to explain that the French cannot tolerate when their heritage is misinterpreted. And between you and me, I don't really know champagne. I drink it. I definitely enjoy it, but not being knowledgeable about something doesn't mean that we can joke about it; it's something we take very seriously. Everything that touches food and wine is very serious in my country. I hope that once you have read my book, you will understand why we are so serious about our food.

When I lived abroad, I not only learnt that we are regarded as arrogant but dirty as well! I learnt a few jokes while in London about French people and how they use soap in their bathroom. But because the subject of this book is not about how many toothbrushes a year French use but more about how we pamper ourselves from the inside, I won't tell you how many showers a week I take. In any case, like all of us, I use perfume, and I take time to choose the one which suits my skin and complexion, whether it replaces my morning shower or not is my business and my secret. In this book, I will reveal many secrets of our art of being French, so please let me keep this one to myself.

Once you know my secrets, you may become a bit more French yourself, not for our arrogance of course, or our hygiene but for our well-being, our little everyday pleasures that make our lives joyful without adding any kilos on our scale. Whether you live in Los Angeles, Alaska or Moscow, you can become a little French yourself. Being French is not only about eating delicious cuisines; it's mainly a question of a lifestyle. We are born to it, so it is easy for us to follow the habits passed on to us for generations, but it is never too late to change the way you live for the better, and it is always a good time to teach good habits to your children. So here it goes – French secrets served on your plate! And as we say in the restaurant industry when we bring customers to their table: 'Please, follow me!'

Part One

THE ART OF BEING FRENCH

Chapter One

FOOD IS SACRED

I N FRANCE, food is a religion. We eat, drink, breathe and think food. We are strict non-vegetarians and love a good *Côte de Boeuf* with a glass of Bordeaux that we take time to enjoy while sitting with friends and family. We favour quality over quantity, always. Most importantly, we choose our wine and meat or fish, we pick and choose our vegetables and we buy fresh food – and I mean it: fresh, i.e., non-processed!

Rule No. 1: Favour Quality over Quantity

You will see how enjoyable it is to go food shopping (or food picking!). Forget about processed items and buy fresh food at the market or in your local shop which sells fresh produce. The French always look for a market wherever they are in the world, and everywhere I've travelled and lived, I found one. Let's not talk about France and Italy, as we are kings of markets, but in other countries like England, Croatia, Greece, Portugal, Germany and Poland, there are markets too, and also outside of Europe, in the US – NYC, San Francisco or Washington – there are markets. Outside of towns, you have local farmers, often even better and cheaper.

While living in London, going to Borough Market was bliss, as well as Kensal Green farmers' market, Chelsea farmers' market and of course Portobello market in my neighbourhood. Some think that buying fresh food or going to a market is more expensive, but I can tell you that it is not true at all. Buying local, from farmers, doesn't cost more, and it's healthier for yourself and the environment. At the local farmer or at the market, you buy less and have less food forgotten at the bottom of your fridge. No more waste and more money in your pocket. When you buy better quality food, fresh food, you pick and choose. It is better for your health, and good health has no price! You also buy less because you need less food to feel full and satisfied.

When in San Francisco, Fort Mason on Sunday morning is great, Ferry building as well and the Mission community market, one of my favourites in my area, at 22nd and Bartlett, every Thursday evening. It's very small, cute and healthy, and you spend a nice time talking to the locals. So let's pretend that you are French and try to go to the market at least once a week, twice even better. Food shopping becomes a real joy when outside, trying samples of food on market stalls, having a chat with the baker, or fishmonger, which is so different to pushing a trolley in a supermarket under neon lights, gallivanting in the Disneyworld of saturated fats and sugar. Sit down even for 10 minutes at a café and have a *petit noir*, enjoy the sun (or the rain) and enjoy your coffee. I've always enjoyed my coffee wherever I was. Farmers markets are not necessarily a guarantee of quality, unfortunately, but you have the right to ask and choose. What you put in your body is of huge importance so you can be picky! Where the farmer is from, where the farm is, what he produces and how the cow that makes your milk has been raised, in what kind of soil he cultivates his carrots... Ask all these questions and you'll always learn new things when talking to farmers, butchers, fish-mongers or cheese producers. Who knows? The butcher could also give you some tips and recipes. Mine is very good and knows how to cook meat perfectly.

NUTRITIONIST'S NOTE

The most basic necessity = being full.

This sentence sums it all up: the higher the quality of the food on your plate, the less of it you eat.

The reverse is also true!

But what does 'quality' really mean?

Simply put, food that contains a maximum of nutrients: vitamins, minerals, enzymes and antioxidants.

These elements must be digestible, and therefore contained in unprocessed food, whether that food is certified organic or not.

The more natural and unprocessed the food is that you digest, the more it will retain its beneficial nutrients.

Try eating the same dish, firstly as a ready-made, processed version and then as a homemade version with organic ingredients cooked at low temperature.

You will see for yourself the incredible difference it makes to your gut, your digestion, your energy and your eating patterns in the hours afterwards.

Never buy too much food. We French want it fresh and we hate waste. It's better to go fresh-food shopping once or twice week than buying half of the supermarket at once. I will guide you through your shopping list later on in this book. Fresh food has higher nutritional value. As said before, you can eat less to feel satisfied. So in the end, it comes cheaper! Buy organic whenever possible. It's a bit more expensive but by buying less and more intelligently will ensure that you save money. Buying better quality food will help save your waistline and your purse strings.

I don't really know what processed food means. Seriously, I've always seen my grandmother, then my mum, cook everything from scratch. Working, raising a child and serving homemade food at the dinner table are not incompatible. As you will discover in these pages, I will give you advice and recipes so you may enjoy cooking and eating like we do in France. You will see that this is all easy. It doesn't take a lot of time, that cooking is pleasure and that you don't have to buy ready-made, processed, unhealthy and ultimately fattening food. It is not a secret that all good restaurants buy high-quality produce!

Take something as delicious as a pancake for instance. After reading this book, seeing how easy it is to make homemade pancakes, you will never buy ready-made pancake boxes again. It is these ready-made supermarket products that add kilos to your weight. There are no chemicals, no added sugar and salt and no fattening, useless products in my kitchen.

The ultimate pancakes:

Preparation: 5 min • Cooking time: 5 min

200g flour	25g melted butter, plus extra for
1½ tsp baking powder	cooking
1 tbsp of sugar	200ml milk
3 eggs	Vegetable oil, for cooking

Mix flour, baking powder, sugar and a pinch of salt in a bowl. Then add eggs, butter and milk. Whisk together by hand or with electric whisk.

Heat a small knob of butter and 1 tsp oil in a pan.

Form pancakes and fry them for 2 minutes on each side.

Quick lactose and sugar-free pancakes!

Preparation: 1 min • Cooking time: 4 min

1 banana mashed	1 egg
1 handful of oats	

Mix all the ingredients in a bowl, heat a frying pan with a bit of coconut or vegetable oil. Put 1tbsp at the time in the pan to form pancakes and fry them for 2 minutes on each side.

Non-processed food doesn't mean cooking a very sophisticated dinner every day. Actually, it's the exact opposite. You can make it simple. Buy good, fresh ingredients. Add some olive oil, garlic, a few herbs, a few spices… Be organised while shopping and cooking to have more time at home, and so, more time for yourself and ultimately more pleasure in your life! There are secrets to cultivating the perfect nutritional diet to allow you to really shine. I will guide you through them and give you more rules to follow but you need to make time for it, every week, just as with all the activities that are important to you! Set aside a space in your daily routine to prepare your 'fuel' for yourself, fuel that will nourish all your cells and become your most important source of energy. Investing in good, fresh, seasonal, unprocessed food is your best investment in life, for life. Your whole being will thank you for it.

Cooking is a great pleasure, and it is not difficult; it's the alarm that awakens all your senses. In France, we take a lot of pleasure to talking about a recipe, a dish we made. We are the kind of people who, while eating lunch, talk about what we're going to eat for dinner.

And with food, we build memories. We all have food memories, not only us French people but everyone around the globe, and that's what makes us all on the same page. It can be a very simple moment, insignificant for others, that stays in our head forever. For me, it's the smell of freshly picked tomato on my dad's small garden, eaten on the way back home; the smell of warm bread in the bakery and half of the baguette eaten straight away; the smell of a tart in the oven; the colours of courgettes; my grandmother making her *gratin de viande* – she passed away 10 years ago but this memory is still vivid in my mind; her *ganses* during the carnival period; the best *jambon-beurre* in the world I had in the brasserie side of a three-Michelin-star restaurant in London (I couldn't afford a three-course meal, but what a sandwich!); the *bagna cauda* (typical niçois dish) that I call my Niçoise revelation – this little start I had when eating it for the first time; the cooking classes in Mexico; the *tajine* learnt in Morocco under a tent; the tons of pasta eaten in Italy; the eggs Benedict, *röti* and *chilaquiles* that I made in restaurant kitchens in London…

The smell of mushrooms that my dad picks every year – we don't know where, as he doesn't want to give up his hidden places in the forest. The wild asparagus that he allowed us to go picking with him, exceptionally sharing his secret spots with me and my family. Life is made of little pleasures: the smell of coffee in the morning, for instance. I love to wake up with this smell and it makes me want to wake up any season of the year. Coffee smell makes you feel cosy in winter and makes you want to have your windows wide open in June, to watch the sun, the flowers, trees or people passing by, to breathe deeply and feel ready for a great day ahead. You see, food is not only about consuming; there is magic in it!

Rule No. 2: Respect the Seasons and Eat Seasonal Food Only

We respect the seasons for anything and everything but first for our food. This is what I've known since I was a child. We eat strawberries in spring. We make salads and cold soups with fresh peas in the summer. I can't wait for June when the fig season starts. I eat them raw or baked. I make jam and salad with rocket and goat cheese... *chicory* (I love *chicory*!) vegetable soups in January and so on... It's just natural. We don't eat strawberries in winter! And we don't buy melon in December! If nature created seasons, it was for a reason.

NUTRITIONIST'S NOTE

Unsuspected hunger

This little-known phenomenon is emerging in developed countries, and has also recently been identified in the US.

It manifests itself as excessive weight gain, even leading to obesity amongst children and adults, who eat large quantities of food and yet are never full!

How is this even possible? Largely because of a severe lack of nutrients. These people are simply not getting enough nutrition; they are severely malnourished.

Deprived of fundamental nutritional elements, the body produces the hormone ghrelin to provoke the person's hunger and thereby causes overeating. To avoid this, there is only one solution: keep watch on the nutritional value of your meal!

Caring about the seasons is the best thing you can do for your palate, your wallet, your health, your weight and for the planet. Fruits in season are so much more desirable, as you have to wait for them. It's like a date.

Anticipation makes it more exciting... We make a wish each time we try a fruit or a vegetable for the first time in the year. It is part of our culture, children and adults alike. When we put the first strawberry of the year to our mouths, we make a wish. Of course, not all wishes are fulfilled, but what the hell! Our hopes and dreams are there. They go along with the perfumes of freshly picked ripe asparagus, blueberries, tomatoes and all seasonal, delightful fruits and vegetables. I put a cherry in my mouth. I close my eyes, and when savouring that very first cherry of the year, I make a wish. That says a lot about our 'we-eat-in-season' philosophy.

When you only eat produce in season, you fill your organism-like batteries for a year because only seasonal food retains all the nutrients which feed your body. Take asparagus, for example; they are so pretty, full of vitamins, nutrients and so short in season... And that's also why we love them so much. They are rare, delicious and so easy to prepare by heating in a pan with olive oil, salt and pepper. That's all you need to reach heaven.

Winter is long, but like each season, it has its own delights. Vegetable soups will highlight, warm up your evenings and fill your apartment with cosy smell of good supper. Spring is coming slowly afterwards, and suddenly, May, my favourite month for what we have on market stalls, like fresh spinach. (Have you ever tried them fresh, cooked with just garlic and olive oil?) The tomatoes start to be dark red and full of juice. The sweet cherries are coming; there is rhubarb to make compote. It's all green and full of colour. It's beautiful and it's again a celebration. The fruits and vegetables are at their best in terms of nutritional value. Their colour and taste are at the peak of their delight. We waited one year to get those amazing strawberries, so let's celebrate and enjoy fully. Strawberries in winter are hard, pale red and tasteless and with no vitamins at all. Strawberries in May are red and juicy. Their flesh is ripe and tender, their perfume sweet. They are full of Vitamin C, crucial to your health and well-being.

Buy from your local producer. Each country grows their own fruits. No need to buy those coming from a remote country in the world.

Fruits and vegetables from farms are at their best. They look imperfectly perfect because they are natural; they taste better and they have kept their vitamins and minerals. So, your body will thank you – and so will the planet, as your bag of fruits won't have done a world tour before landing on your plate. This is also why going to a market or to your local shop which sells fresh produce, as opposed to a supermarket with processed food, is so important. As said earlier, if you eat quality food, i.e. fresh and seasonal, you will eat produce full of nutritional value.

Therefore, you will eat less and you will feel full and satisfied after your meal. We are lucky, as there has been an important organic – buying seasonal – short-circuit trend for a few years in many countries, which is great, as that's all I've known since my childhood. We've always been naturally trendy in France. Am I being arrogant again?

Chapter Two

GROWING UP IN FRANCE

G ROWING UP in France is having a croissant before and after school, getting homemade soup almost 12 months a year and a drop of red wine in your water on special occasions. This drop of wine is something normal in my family and I don't remember anyone arguing with it, ever. That drop of wine coloured my water and made me feel like a grown-up woman who drank a very good wine, which I found, even at the time, very classy. Growing up in France, it's developing some food habits from your mum that she got from her mum, etc. ... It's being obliged to try some food before saying that we don't like it, trying new things, having a great variety of dishes and learning to be curious about food. Eating at the table and taking time and pleasure to eat, talking about food, thanking your mum and dad for their cooking, asking questions about new recipes. We eat three times a day and always seated. We learn from our early days to take the time to eat properly at regular times, not doing anything else but eating during our meal.

Rule No. 3: Sit Down and Take Time to Eat

The French don't want to be bothered during their lunch break; even if it is only half an hour, it has to be a sacred half an hour. No phone, no computer, no reading, nothing but us with food and colleagues... maybe. Not rushing and being focused on our food helps to appreciate what we do. This is a very important moment we take to recharge our batteries and refuel our bodies with quality food, even if this food is just a sandwich or a simple salad. I respect food. I respect my grandmother's, aunt's and mum's dishes. I wouldn't even think about missing a family Sunday lunch. Sunday lunch is an opportunity to gather with family that we often mix with friends, and an opportunity to stay around the table for long hours, dip our bread in the roast dish, finish a bottle of wine, open another one, laugh and enjoy the moment. Life is short, and the French know it. Family and friends' gatherings have always been happy events in my family. And noisy too! There are not a lot of us, but enough to be loud. When we are together there's always homemade food, wine and/or champagne, an aperitif, a three-course meal (with cheese in between) and a lot of laughter. Singing and dancing occur very often too. A good meal is divine and for us, it's natural to let it go and relax from starter to dessert.

One of my non-French friends was making dinner once just for herself in my kitchen. She broke eggs in a bowl, mixed them and poured them into a frying pan. Waiting in the living room and not seeing her coming to enjoy her omelette at the table, I went back to the kitchen and saw her finishing her plate standing in front of the sink. I was very surprised and worried for her digestion as engulfing an omelette in front of the sink while facing the wall is not good for the body. I wanted to tell her that it doesn't take that much time to reach the dining room, sit down and peacefully eat an omelette. Actually, it may take 25 minutes, cooking and eating. Altogether, her digestion would have gone smoother. Her brain would stop being harassed by all kinds of thoughts she could have while enjoying a wonderful omelette. (I would have added some fresh herbs and a bit of cheese, but this is just my French taste.) Her body would be fuelled for the rest of her day.

NUTRITIONIST'S NOTE

The Vegetative Nervous System: why you should stop to eat

In France, people stop to eat; we sit down, rest for a moment and dedicate our full attention to the food. There is a little-known reason behind this ancestral practice: the changing state of our vegetative nervous system, that is, whether it is active or resting. When in action mode, your body's biology changes: the orthosympathetic system promotes alertness and blood flow to the muscles (just like during sport).

When you are calm and relaxed, blood instead flows to the organs in the abdomen, particularly those involved in the digestion process (the liver, pancreas, intestine, stomach, etc.) This is the parasympathetic system, which also activates secretions necessary for digestion.

Just think about your last sports session: you didn't feel hungry during the actual exercise... You'll soon notice a difference in the quality of your digestion if you take a proper break for meals!

My mum makes great gnocchi. I absolutely love it and have eaten gnocchi from an early age. Growing up, I asked her to show me how to make gnocchi and roll them on the back of a fork to make those little stripes on each one. Since then, we always make them on a very old wooden irregular and ruffled board that belonged to my great-grand-mother who was the Italian mamma with grey hair pulled up in a bun and always wearing a black shawl. You understand why I could never buy ready-made gnocchi in a supermarket; not only they are easy to make and when homemade have more nutritional value, but they also bring back all these wonderful memories I built over the years in my family. You might have similar memories from your family, or if you don't, it is never too late to build your memories with your children. One day, they will remember these sweet moments when you made your gnocchi or other dishes together and will thank you!

Growing up in France is also to learn to cook from a young age. I was the sous-chef of my mum for a long time, picking parsley, peeling pota-toes and, as I was growing up, got more responsibilities like following a recipe to make a *gâteau au yaourt* and so on... I am still her sous-chef but now she's mine sometimes too, and we both enjoy it immensely. My niece was my sous-chef when she was a child. She is now 17 and loves cooking and eating homemade food.

Growing up in France is also going to the beach with a whole picnic fit for a king (and not just a bag of crisps and a bottle of soda). The potato omelette from my grandmother with a Niçoise salad, some fruits and water carried for kilometres in the cooler to reach the beach on foot. It's my grandfather forcing me to eat persimmon that he liked very ripe and gave to me with a teaspoon, as it was so runny. I didn't like it at the time; actually, the texture made me feel sick, but now I eat it, and every time I see a persimmon, I think about my grandfather. It's the same with pine nuts: we used to go on the steps next to his house, under a pine tree, and in season, we picked the cones. He broke them with a hammer and gave me the pine nuts to savour. His homemade ravioli that he made by the hundreds, spread on two single beds put together as the kitchen was far too small, that I pilfered and ate raw with my cousin. The cherries engulfed, perched on the tree, the smell of onion grilled by my mum, the famous *pâte au pistou* and the *ragoût* of my dad.

Fizzy drinks: addictions – insulin & dehydration

I'll be blunt here; fizzy drinks have no place in a healthy, nutritious diet. They should be relegated to the 'never consume' category, right up there with sweets! Why? Due to their composition, they are a real ticking time bomb. Even if they are 'light', it has been proven that sweeteners cause the pancreas to secrete insulin, just as if the drink contained real sugar.

In the classic version of a fizzy drink, one can contains on average seven sugar cubes (This is the exact case with Coca-Cola.) The gases they contain quickly release acids into the body and disturb the digestive physiology as well as cause dehydration. Finally, their chemical additives are known to be carcinogenic, neurotoxic, endocrine disruptors... and addiction is, of course, the final trap.

Natural alternatives exist: fruit kefir and kombucha are both fizzy and revitalising whilst still respecting your health.

Rule No. 4: No Sodas or Coke, Just 1.5 Litres of Water

We learn from an early age that sodas are not good and that the secret of living well with a good complexion and fewer wrinkles is to drink a lot of water – and wine. It was strange to see toddlers munching on crisps and drinking fizzy drinks in foreign countries I have visited. Those mini, individual chips bags I had never seen before. Chips are full of bad fats and salt, sodas are full of sugar; both very unhealthy for children. They develop bad food habits which will last into their adulthood and damage their health and teeth.

A simple baguette with a bar of dark chocolate or any fruit with a bottle of water would make a better afterschool *goûter* than chips and soda. Eating habits are crucial and we learn how to eat well from early childhood, and again, it is never too late to change.

I only have water while eating – and wine. I don't do coke or sodas at mealtimes. Actually, we rarely drink fizzy stuff except champagne. Sodas have too many calories, too much sugar, and we wouldn't have enough space for our patisseries dear to our hearts. It's also a question of habit; I always have my bottle of water or mug or thermos with me. I've never had any soda at the table with my parents. It was water only. I didn't learn to like fizzy drinks when I was a child because I had no opportunity to taste them. I only had the choice between still water or sparkling water and it was not questioned, as it was the only option I had at home. My body didn't get used to having all this sugar at once, and because I was not used to it when I was a child, I don't like it as an adult. Children who drink sugary drinks during their meals fill their bodies with sugar and don't have enough space for good quality, nutritional food. They often leave good nutrition on their plate and, despite leaving the table satisfied, are hungry again in no time. And yet again, they eat sugary things in between meals. The vicious circle of bad habits starts at an early age. Later on in their lives, they will start dieting to lose weight, adding fuel to the vicious circle. Dieting helps to lose weight only temporarily; solely good habits prevent weight gain and are life-lasting.

NUTRITIONIST'S NOTE

Water is not a food

Water is the only element of daily consumption that is not a food.

It is used to flush the body of its waste products, to maintain a good circulation of liquids (blood, lymph, bile, etc.) and to transport nutrient molecules to our cells.

Ideally, it should not be consumed, or should be consumed very little with food, because a large glass of water will dissolve the precious digestive juices... Thus, hello bloating, heaviness and poor nutritional assimilation.

Outside of meals, however, drink it without moderation!

If you want a little liquid during your meal, a small cup of hot water, tea or fruity herbal tea will help your digestion.

French women drink champagne and wine but we also drink a lot of water. Drinking water, especially in between meals, is very important. Actually, it's a necessity. I personally start my day with a mug of hot water with the juice of one lemon and some ginger. If I haven't got a lemon, at least a glass of hot water. Our body absorbs Vitamin C better on an empty stomach. You'll be hydrated as soon as out of bed, which is good for the body and the skin. The body is composed of 60% water. Drinking water helps with digestion, circulation, absorption, maintenance of body temperature, creation of saliva... It protects your tissue, spinal cord and joints. It helps to excrete waste through perspiration, urination and defecation, helps with the absorption of nutrients and keeps the skin bright.

Not being well hydrated can cause a reduction of motivation, increase fatigue and make exercise (both physically and mentally) feel much more difficult. The brain is also strongly influenced by hydration. When you feel tired and feel like drinking coffee to wake you up, drink a good glass of water instead. You will see how fast your fatigue will go. Drinking plenty of water may help prevent and relieve constipation.

Should we carry on explaining how important water is? Soda and juices can hydrate a tiny bit but also add more kilos on your scale and cause all the damage mentioned already.

Water also helps to prevent hangovers. Alcohol is a diuretic, so it makes you lose more water than you take in.

Dehydration causes symptoms like thirst, fatigue and a dry mouth. Drinking a glass of water in between each glass of wine is a good way to reduce a hard and very unpleasant wakeup. Drinking at least 1.5 litres of water a day is the best way to stay hydrated and lose weight. Water intake can also increase satiety. Research on 50 women who were overweight showed that drinking 500ml of water three times a day and before meals led to significant body weight loss.

When dehydrated, the skin can become more vulnerable to premature wrinkling. Conclusion: let's drink a lot of water. It is as simple as that. Drink a lot of water, even though you don't feel like it. Fix yourself some goals and force yourself a bit. Once your body has got used to it, it will naturally long for more water, and you'll feel thirsty more often. Motivate yourself, find your way, look at your 1.5-litre bottle of water in the morning and let her know she'll be finished by the evening (that's what I do and it works). We live in harmony with our bodies in France and according to a principle, *homo sum: humani nihil a me alienum puto.* (I am human and nothing human is alien to me.) Observe your body. Learn to understand and to listen to it. Once it starts functioning like a well-oiled machine, it will tell you when you have eaten too much, when you need to eat or that you need vegetables or water.

For water, if your pee no longer has any smell or colour during the day, it means that you have drunk enough. You may continue drinking water if you still need it, of course. As said, water is excellent for our body! Children are served water in France from their early days. Waiters bring water to the table without any question. It's part of our education, and I love to add a few slices of lemon and/or cucumber in my bottle in the summer, or peach slices or a few strawberries. Drinking water can be fun too!

Chapter Three

THE FRENCH WOMAN

THE FRENCH woman drinks wine, smokes if she wants to and doesn't care about what other people think as long as it doesn't spoil her pleasure. She also knows that food is food and junk is junk – no association between the two. We eat a lot of vegetable soups and we don't classify pizza as vegetable simply because there is tomato on it. A pizza is a pizza, so when we decide to eat one, we enjoy it like there is no tomorrow, and when tomorrow comes, we go for a salad with a glass of rosé and a long walk.

Rule No.5: Balance Your Meals

This is one of our best-kept secrets. Most people think that we eat everything and stay slim. It is true, but if we eat a very big meal one day, we eat a much lighter meal the following day. And we go for a walk. Basically, meat, cheese, potatoes one day, followed by rice, vegetables and salad the next day. A wine and cheese platter is a necessity for us, especially shared between girls at *apéro* time. As mentioned before, we would just eat more vegetables the next day and go for a long walk. I love walking. Paris is a walkable city and most Parisians go out for a walk after each meal. It is called a digestive walk. It doesn't need to be a long walk equipped with full gear, sticks, trainers, backpack, etc. ... You can simply go out wearing your heels or flats; whatever you fancy and makes you feel pretty and good. Well, before it was discovered that one should walk 10,000 steps a day to remain healthy, we were doing it all naturally in France. We are lucky in Nice because we have the sea; walking by the sea every day is a must. But everywhere in the world, there are spots for walking. Just walk whenever you can and wherever you are, especially after your meals. If you go shopping for fresh food several times a week, it will also help you to get those steps in. This is especially so if you are organised with your shopping: you won't need to carry heavy bags, just a few fresh ingredients in your nice basket during a nice little walk. I will help you to get organised with your shopping later on.

Walking also decreases stress and anxiety levels and boosts creativity by reducing brain fog. When we need a break, the best thing to do is to go for a walk and come back with a refreshed body and brain. It is proven that it's like a workout at the gym. Taking a walk will get the blood flowing, help to relax and maintain a high heart rate without running. I hate running, so to compensate, I walk a lot. I do that for myself first. I found my way to take control of my life and my health, and I love this idea. I also save money on buses, taxis, petrol for my car, and on top of that, I help the planet to breathe better too. Isn't that beautiful?

To conciliate my body with my soul, I also practise yoga. I found it a bit boring at the beginning to be honest, but when I found the right teacher a few years ago, it changed completely the way I feel my body, the way I breathe and the way I see yoga.

I practised dance for a long time. I don't have as much time to do so anymore, but my body feels the need to move regularly, as it's used to it, so when in need, I go for a walk or dance in my kitchen! It is important to find your own most pleasurable sport. If it is dance, go for it. If it is swimming, go for swimming. If you take pleasure in moving your body, you will not have to force yourself to do it and your body will reclaim it. You will not even notice that you are making an effort. Effortless sport? Yes, anything you do for pleasure is effortless, even sport; this is how I see it!

Above all, remember: cheat days are allowed! I never feel guilty. Why? Because I know I have good eating habits. We always have greens on our table, our famous green salad with vinaigrette at the end of our meal! I always have more vegetables on my plate than carbs or proteins. You may start changing your habits by putting vegetables on your plate first, leaving only a small place for proteins or carbs. Once you have eaten what you had on your plate, end your meal with a green salad with vinaigrette. We do it all the time! And don't forget to go for a digestive walk after your meal whenever you can. You will soon realise that you feel much better. I walk and I drink water... a lot. Guilt is not part of a French woman's vocabulary, as it's unhealthy. I can drink champagne at breakfast just because I fancy it with a *tartine* of butter and jam, why not?

Rule No. 6: Boost Your Self-Esteem by Taking Care of Your Appearance

Life is short and being healthy and pretty every day is important; it makes our lives more joyful and our self-esteem stronger. That's why we pay attention to our appearance every day and not only when we go out in the evening. A bit of makeup every day versus a bit more and never too much when we go out is our way to feel pretty – always. How could we be generous and considerate toward people without feeling well in ourselves first? Feeling healthy and pretty go together. Shoes are very often heels because this makes our legs longer and our figure slender. We all have that little black dress in our wardrobe, the one that works for any occasion and is elegant with flats as well. We don't wear leggings except to exercise. That's what they are made for. We would never think about running errands wearing yoga leggings. Never!

We dress every day. We don't need to put on our best clothes. We dress comfortably but we make an effort each day because we know how important it is to look good. Looking good makes us feel better and more comfortable in our own skin. Feeling pretty gives us the feeling that we can achieve anything. Confidence is the key. So I always dress, even simply: a cotton dress, or trousers with a T-shirt. Add some colour with simple jewels even whilst going to the grocery shop. I feel more confident and I can choose better what I need in the grocery shop when I feel good and pretty. I can say yes or no to whoever I want and, in those circumstances to the shopkeeper, and ultimately spend less money because I buy strictly what I need.

We also match our bras and panties even when we are single (or actually even more when we are single – why wouldn't we?!) Again, it's a question of feeling good, feeling sexy and how important this is for our mood, brain and well-being. A balanced life equals a balanced scale. I look after myself for myself first. Getting a manicure is another must, but not the French one. For some reason, the French manicure is worn by every girl but the French. I personally keep my nails short and well filed, with red or dark red polish that I unfortunately have to remove when I am working (for hygiene), but as soon as I have a day off, I paint my nails and I even go for a coral or pink in the summer when I am a bit tanned. My skin routine is very easy and affordable. I can tell you that I tried a lot of different brands and different natural techniques to look after myself, and the best for my skin is summed up in the words: dry brushing, massage and moisturising. First thing in the morning, I dry-brush my skin for around 20 seconds. You can buy a special small wooden brush with natural bristles that does the job perfectly, and it allows me to go on every single little corner of my face and neck. Then I spray with a toner (a geranium-based one suggested by my yoga teacher). Then I massage my face for around one minute with either avocado oil or carrot oil, feeling my face and myself invigorated, and I finish with a simple moisturiser cream. That's all. I don't spend too much money on products, and my skin looks fresh. When I go to the beauty salon (around once a year), the beautician doesn't want to give me a deep cleaning as she says I don't need it, thanks to my beauty routine.

Between you and me, I hate washing my hair, so I've decided to offer myself the luxury of going to the hairdresser once a week for a wash and a blow-dry. I found a good hairdresser in my neighbourhood who does the job the way I like it: fast and well while I am reading my magazine. It's a bit expensive, but my confidence, well-being and time are worth it. And I don't spend money on expensive shampoo or a hairdryer that I don't know how to use anyway! I walk to my hairdresser and back, of course, as I walk to the market, and on my way back, I stop for a coffee – we all do it in France. We drink our coffee black, short – no milk froth, cinnamon or pumpkin spices during Halloween season. A coffee is a coffee, preferably with no sugar to feel the real taste.

Rule No. 7: Enjoy Life's Pleasures, Enjoy Your Food Without Feeling Guilty.

It is a known phenomenon in France that guilt is a stress factor which can have a bad influence on your digestion. Feeling bad, guilty and skipping a meal are a sure way to end up indulging in junk food.

It is easy to create a vicious circle when you eat your food feeling guilty. You then try to compensate and not eat at all. Your body will demand more food afterwards and will store it for later, adding kilos to your weight. If you regularly eat good quality, homemade food, you will not have to feel guilty. Feeding yourself, taking pleasure in it, will be part of your good routine and healthy habits; guilt will disappear.

Mindful eating for better digestion

Eating for joy and pleasure, without guilt, affects our waistlines much less than excessive control and deprivation.

This may seem contradictory, but in order to understand this, we must remember a notion that is rarely discussed in nutrition: the ingrained memory of starvation. In the 2.5 million years that humans have been on Earth, they have lived 99% of that time in a context where food was not abundant and regular.

Eating three times a day, as in France, is a very recent phenomenon in human history. This means that when you are in 'diet' mode, feeling frustrated and restricted, your brain goes into storage mode.

However, if you eat when you are hungry (not more often than this, of course), with a contented acceptance that you are eating because you need to, your body will burn many more calories and better assimilate nutrients.

The French sometimes eat raw meat (with an egg yolk on the top. Can you believe it? It's called steak tartare). We do enjoy snails (but with butter and garlic only), frogs' legs and *foie gras*. Yes, we do! We eat a lot of cheese. We have something like 1200 kinds...

It takes a lot of eating to choose your favourite ones. And we try it again and again with a glass of red wine. Because we favour quality over quantity, and we don't feel guilty whilst eating – on the contrary, we believe it's one of life's greatest pleasures (I did say one of them, yes!) – we eat without thinking about tomorrow, and we eat less. Our body would tell us once we have eaten enough and we wouldn't touch another piece of this cheese until our next meal.

Food is crucial for our living and health. We cannot possibly feel guilty feeding ourselves. Instead, we take pleasure in this vital activity. French women think that talking about food while on a date is very sexy. It happened to me many times. Drinking champagne too, of course!

Chapter Four

THE FRENCH DIET

L ET'S FACE it; if dieting worked, the whole world would be slim already. So why do we keep on doing the same thing expecting a different result? Diets do a lot of collateral damage, and as early as on young children. It's horrifying but statistics show that in the US, 80% of 10-year-old girls have already been on a diet. Over the past 25 years, the age has dropped. In 1970, the average-age girl began dieting was 14, which was already tragic. Diets often provoke what we call a yoyo effect, losing and then gaining more weight once the diet is over, so people have to diet again, and thus begins a vicious circle.

We don't diet in France. We simply eat fresh, balanced food at regular mealtimes – three to four times a day.

Rule No. 8: Have Only Three or Maximum Four Meals a Day, Always Seated

You may have observed during your travels in France that streets are emptier during our mealtimes. This is because everybody is busy eating. Breakfast when you wake up and lunch always between 12:30 and 2:30 p.m. We stop all for our dinner between 7 p.m. and 9 p.m. Most restaurants are closed between 3 and 7 p.m. All best restaurants are closed in between meals. We may stay at our table for longer, enjoy our last glass of wine but kitchens will close at 3 p.m. after lunch and no more orders after 10 pm. Lunch break is a sacred time even during a busy day of work. You recharge your batteries, and you are more productive afterwards, your digestion works better if you stop and sit down to eat. When children come from school, a light *goûter* may become our fourth meal. I still have a *goûter* very often even, though I haven't been a child for a while! But no chips or sodas, a plain croissant or *pain au chocolat*, a pancake, homemade of course, a piece of dark chocolate, a fruit and some water. A herbal tea will feed you and your children much better without damaging your digestive patterns. Our body gets used to regular meals, always at the same time. Again, the digestion works better when we eat regular meals. Our body functions as a well-oiled machine; our intestines, so crucial for digestion and our immunity, need this regularity and the time between our meals to work properly.

During my travels, I saw some people eating their food in just a few minutes. Just one dish and a soda – no green leaves, no vegetables, no wine, no water… Someone I knew very often skipped meals and ate only two or three real meals per week. Yes, per week. Instead, he would sometimes eat two plain pieces of white bread (you know, the square one that tastes like nothing) just because he was lazy or broke (as he said). I don't think that lazy and broke are excuses to treat yourself that way. It takes no time to assemble some vegetables to make a salad or even (if you are very lazy) to eat a ripe tomato just like that, as an apple, and it doesn't cost much, as the price of a tomato is cheaper than a bag of bread. Filling your body with no nutrients, just carbs, and skipping meals is a very bad habit that needs to be changed in order to improve health.

You have understood by now that food is a religion in France, and we do enjoy it! We take care to prepare our food from fresh produce. Our plate is balanced with vegetables, proteins and/or carbs. We take time to eat and enjoy our plate without feeling bad whilst we eat, and we leave the table satisfied. Because our produce is full of nutritional value, we eat less and don't feel hungry for a while after having left the table. Some people who come to France say that our portions are small. They may be smaller but they contain everything one needs to have pleasure, feel full and be contented. A slice of baguette with a piece of camembert or comté cheese to finish our meal will definitely satisfy any cravings, and it is much healthier than a packet of biscuits between lunch and dinner. The secret to fitting in my skinny jeans is to eat quality food, balanced with ripe vegetables and fruits, and to sit down to three or four meals a day and leave the table satisfied. I don't need to snack in between my meals because I don't feel hungry. Eating tasteless food or unripe fruits frustrate people who then compensate and relieve this frustration by snacking on the first pack of biscuits they see.

Rule No. 9: No Snacking in Between Meals

Snacking in between meals is one of the worst things for our weight. If you leave your table satisfied and you eat three, maximum four, times a day, you will soon realise how easy it is to refuse that poor-quality chocolate or those biscuits in between meals and how easy it will become to ignore those greasy, salty chips at a cocktail party – no unhealthy hunger, good digestion, no temptation.

The whole world knows that French don't just eat carrots and broccoli. So why don't we gain weight even when we do eat fries cooked in duck fat? First, fries in duck fat are insanely good and we enjoy insanely good homemade food. Second, we don't do that every day. Third, when we do that, we have no frustration, no guilt (rule no. 7) because again, we know that we do have a good food pattern. We add meat to our vegetables and not the opposite. We eat regularly, three to four times a day maximum (rule no. 8). And we feel satisfied when we leave our table, so we don't do any snacking in between the meals (rule no. 9). Balance is the key. The body doesn't like drama but consistency. Including several food groups (proteins, slow-burn sugars, fats) to provide your body with a varied supply of nutrients and a digestive synergy will stabilise your blood sugar level and reduce any food cravings in the following hours. You'll protect yourself from over-stimulating digestive juice and enzymes that can lead to cholesterol and blood-sugar-level problems, and of course, excessive weight.

NUTRITIONIST'S NOTE

How to better digest fats

First of all, it is important to distinguish between good fats and bad fats. In the 1980s and '90s, everyone saw fats as being responsible for excess weight. Today, we know that this is not only false but also that low-fat products can cause the opposite reaction to what is expected, sometimes with more calories.

In contrast, cold-pressed vegetable oils, seeds, avocado and oily fish offer sources of fat that have been scientifically proven to have positive health benefits. Of course, the fat found in chicken skin, beef and cheese are also very tempting... So what can we do to digest these fats better?

A simple solution will save both your digestion and your figure; put some greens on your plate!

Fibre, oxygenating chlorophyll, alkalising minerals... all these will lower the acidity of fatty foods, boost your digestive enzymes and slow down the absorption of fats.

A top tip: a good way to find your balance, once your food patterns have become regular, is to give yourself permission to eat until you are satisfied. You first need to figure out what makes you feel good and what makes you feel bad. Once you know your body, things will become simple; you will eat things which make your body feel good and avoid things which make you feel lousy. Listen to your body – to your guts, in other words, not to your tongue and throat. Your tongue and throat would tell you to eat five kilos of chocolate and cakes. Don't listen to them but go deeper in your body. Listen to your stomach, to your guts; they will tell you the truth. You will know what your body needs. Work with your appetite instead of fearing it, and eat mindfully. In France, we *prevent* weight gain instead of *promoting* weight loss. As per our food patterns, we are used to balancing our life with good food. We really enjoy what we eat, while knowing that it's good for our health makes us consider food in a totally different way. We know that when excess weight is added to our body, it's more difficult (and even more when we are ageing) to lose it. Making some tweaks for a better quality of life, enjoying the food we eat without putting on weight is far easier than putting on weight and then trying desperately to lose it.

Happy eaters are less inclined to food binge. Light or diet food is not healthy. We know that, and between a few things known for being fattening, research shows that among light chips, marshmallow, camembert and *cassoulet*, well... the light chips are the worst. They contain 482 calories per 100g, which is a lot. Then comes the marshmallows, camembert, and the winner with less fat is *cassoulet*.

So if you want advice from a French woman who loves cheese, when you have *une petite faim*, eat a piece of bread with camembert. If you really fancy that cheese plate at the restaurant, go for it and eat a lot of vegetables the following day (and go for a walk just afterwards) but please, let's forget about the light, low-calorie stuff, as that is terrible. Eat well. Keep the balance between the heavier stuff (like cheese) and easily digestible food (fish, for example). Always remember to add vegetables to your diet. Again and again, eat homemade, non-processed food; you will feel better and lighter.

Think twice before buying a bag of nachos. Let's be clear: putting a bag of nachos and cheese in the microwave is not cooking.

I realised when talking with people that a lot of them think that they eat well but still can't lose weight... Let's have an experiment: eat the way you are used to for a week and make a note of EVERYTHING, from breakfast to the last bit of chocolate in front of TV in the evening. Count the snacks. Count how many cups of coffee, tea, glasses of water or soda... Being more aware of what you do consume will help you to start realising that you either eat too much or not enough of something.

Then you can start to balance and your new life will begin. A bit more French, of course!

Again, balance is the key. Start from the beginning. Your body needs to change its habits. First, by eating smaller portions. Serving your meal in a small plate or bowl can help a lot. Smaller portions of quality food will fill you up better than huge portions of poor-quality, processed food and make you stop snacking. Start serving the vegetables first, and only then add the carbs or proteins. Always eat more broccoli than chicken or more mixed salad than pasta. Make eating time a celebration. Choose your favourite bowl or plate. (I sometimes drink some water or *kombucha* in a champagne glass as it's nicer.) Make it yours. Celebrate in it!

NUTRITIONIST'S NOTE

Digestion starts with the eyes

It's hard to believe, but it's true!

Things we see are always linked to sensory memories, which form a database of bodily responses to these things.

When we see certain foods, this associative memory is transmitted to the brain through the optic nerve and activates emotions, desires or feelings of distaste.

In the case of a dish that you love, your digestive system will begin its work immediately upon seeing the food, starting with a sure sign: salivation.

Hence the expression, "I put on weight just by looking at cake!"

If you have ever found yourself salivating at just the sight of a roast chicken, a cake fresh from the oven or any other favourite dish, you now know why!

Rule No. 10: Eat Slowly and Chew Well.

We don't even think about this in France. We take our time to eat. The French on average spend two hours and 11 minutes at the table each day. We love staying long hours and talking at our dinner table, talking about food whilst eating, of course!

When I was a child, I was a difficult baby according to my mum, meaning I cried a lot except when I was eating... It was a sign, maybe... I've always been slow at the table. I was known for that and known to stock my food in my mouth between my gums and cheeks before swallowing. I then inherited the nickname 'hamster'... Without behaving like a hamster, it's important to take it slow, being conscious that you have to slow down the pace, put the fork down when eating and allow yourself time for chewing when your fork is down. It will become natural, a habit with time and very soon you won't have to think about it anymore.

The vagus nerve is the longest of the 12 cranial nerves. The name 'vagus' means 'wandering' in Latin, as it reaches most of the body's organs. It also runs from the brain to part of the colon and sends signals in both directions. It affects how hungry and how full we are. When we eat, the food gets into the stomach and guts. That's when it starts to release satiety hormones which feed back to the brain to tell us we're full. But that food needs to be chewed and processed a little bit. We need to start absorbing the glucose from the food, and that happens somewhere between 5 and 20 minutes whilst we are chewing. When the glucose in the body goes up, the insulin senses this and insulin goes up as well. Satiety hormones from the guts are released. All this goes back to the brain and says that we are full.

Eating fast doesn't give enough time for the brain to get the signal, so people carry on eating when they shouldn't. If the food goes down to the stomach in big lumps, with little chewing, it will be difficult to digest and make you feel heavy and ingest more food than needed. Eating slowly helps to chew better and therefore helps the digestive process. By eating slowly, you recognise the food, appreciate the texture, savour the experience and get your body to recognise when you're full.

As soon as we start to think or look at some food, we salivate. The saliva contains enzymes that break the food down and moisten the mouth for easier swallowing. Nature is well made, no? It's proven: eating fast without being focused on what we are doing adds stress and eventually weight to our scale. When you eat slowly and mindfully, you digest better and can lose and maintain your good weight.

Making good-looking food is also very important. Add colour to your table and make your plate look pretty, even if you are on your own. The famous expression, "We eat with our eyes first," has been proven, and research shows that eating is a multi-sensorial experience. Sight and smell are as important as the taste. The hot croissant's smell while passing by the local bakery is always in my mind wherever I am. Living abroad, I happened to have tears in my eyes while passing by a shop and smelling those *viennoiseries* freshly out of the oven that reminded me of my favourite bakery in Nice. The coffee just ground, the chicken roasting at the butcher's window, the vision of a big creamy chocolate cake or a stall full of red fruits... these make all our senses awaken... The biting, chewing parts are an important part of digestion but the visual cues can alter the perception of smell and flavour and help the digestion process.

A professor of experimental psychology at Oxford showed that the eyes lead and the tongue follows; we see the food and the brain tells us what to expect. That's why the look of our table and plate is very important. We do think about our plate's aesthetics in France, again all naturally, a fresh table cloth, a nice plate, a matching napkin, fresh flowers on the table, a sprinkle of parsley or cilantro on the top of your dishes, spices, grains, a drizzle of olive oil and a slice of lemon are those little things that will make your food even more enjoyable and more easily digestible.

Chapter Five

WINE AND THE FRENCH PARADOX

I'VE MENTIONED champagne a lot so far in this book. This is because I drink it, in fact, on any occasion! I drink champagne when I am happy, when I am sad, when I have something to celebrate or even to celebrate the fact that I don't have anything to celebrate, when it's my birthday of course, but also my non-birthday and when it's a full moon... Wine and champagne are very important in our lives because life needs to be celebrated.

There are two types of wine – French wines and wines from the rest of the world. I know this is a little pretentious again! France and Italy are the biggest wine producers. France doesn't go without wine, and wine doesn't go without France. It's an unsociable relationship. As Michel Bouvier (a biochemist) once said: "Humans created wine, a long time ago, from the fruit of the vine and they were so proud of their invention that they made it not only an important part of their food supply but also integrated it in religion, traditions, pleasure and even culture." Wine has long been recommended as a more hygienic drink than water because water could be soiled by disease. The alcohol present in could purify the wine from bacteria and viruses. Well... hundreds of years later, the French still think the same. Especially when drinking strong alcohol like a *digestif* after a big dinner, we say in my family that it pushes the food down and makes us digest better as well as killing diseases.

The history of many French wineries dates to Roman times when the southern shores were Greek in the sixth century BC. Viticulture flourished with the founding of the Greek colony of Marseille; the French made it a part of their civilisation and still consider winemaking an art and a lifestyle. Economic decline in Europe and two world wars stopped the wine industry for decades and competition threatened French brands such as Champagne and Bordeaux. This led to new laws in 1935 to defend French interests and heritage, so the AOC was born: *Appellation d'Origine Contrôlée*. France counts 76,000 vineyards and produces between 50 and 60 million hectolitres per year, or seven to eight billion bottles. It means a lot of wine drinking, not only in France, of course, but we do drink wine with our meals. We cannot deny it. So yet again, how do we remain healthy and svelte? Quality over quantity is the answer here. We respect wine, also because it is a very special and very old nectar, so we savour it as opposed to binge-drinking. Just one or two glasses at our dinner table or lunch of good-quality wine will do no harm. On the contrary, except for a very few occasions – but then again, for several days afterwards, we will be drinking a lot of water and walking.

NUTRITIONIST'S NOTE

The bright side of wine

Often caught in the crossfire of opinions, wine is a delicate subject. Those against it point out wine's harmful effects on health, while those who love it cannot dissociate wine from a perfect festive meal. And to top it all off, French cuisine, with its exceptional winemaking traditions and its consideration of gastronomy as art, is inseparable from this intoxicating nectar. What if, for once, we talk about the good qualities of wine and its positive effects? First of all, wine has been used for millennia to preserve and enhance traditional remedies. It has played a large part in medicine and healthcare throughout the ages.

Moreover, red wine has properties that are highly valued today, and it is the only substance that can claim to possess these health powers. Its anthocyanins have been shown to slow the formation of atheromatous plaques. The polyphenols that make up its composition increase antioxidant levels within two to four hours after the meal – hello youth! An unoxidised cell is a little bit of vitality gained.

France is the source of many grape varieties (such as cabernet sauvignon, chardonnay, pinot noir, sauvignon blanc and syrah) that are now planted throughout the world as well as winemaking practices and styles of wine that have been adopted in other producing countries. Champagne as well as French wines gets the appellation AOC. That's why I'm going back to the champagne episode in my first chapter to prove not that I am not arrogant but why a bubbly wine or Prosecco cannot be called champagne. Champagne is an appellation AOC that designates a white bubbly wine exclusively elaborated in France, in the Champagne region, according to methods strictly defined by law.

Saying that champagne is French is a pleonasm and using the name 'champagne' to qualify a fizzy wine from another country would be an abusive use of the AOC. Champagne is French, no contestation!

Wine is something so complex to comprehend that just a few people on the globe can say that they know it very well. When we talk about wine, we talk about the grape, the region, sub-region, the rain, the wine producer, the barrel in which it will age and how long it will age, the colour, the bottle, the appellation and the cork; everything is important and will make wine unique. It's fascinating. The vine is very dependent on the environment, land, climate and exposition, which is the incline of the land. Land which is depleted in organic material, porous and well drained will give rich and concentrated wines, whereas well-watered soil will give an abundant harvest but diluted wine.

NUTRITIONIST'S NOTE

The bright side of wine

What, another surprise? Red wine is proven to have antimicrobial effects in the mouth... amazing, isn't it? Who would have thought that wine prevented cavities?

Its protection of the cardiovascular system is also one of wine's best-known qualities, thanks to the polyphenols it contains.

According to a study in the *Journal of Gastroenterology*, people who drink red wine have a healthier and more diverse microbiome than those who don't. This is believed to be due to the polyphenols present in raisin skins, which is the preferred fuel for gut bacteria.

Aside from the land, man's part is very important in vines' quality. Man looks after the land and will chose the best period for the wine harvest. Wine is made of what nature gave us: soil, fruits, water and sun. The vinification, or winemaking, is the process of transforming the grapes into wine. Formerly obscure and secret, it's nowadays more known and mastered. And even though science and technology occupy a big part of the cellar, the vignerons' *savoir-faire* will determine the wine signature. For its ageing, the wine needs a lot of attention but especially a good environment. The conservation of temperature, the humidity level of the room and the air circulation shouldn't be tampered with. And then, finally, the tasting comes. Sight, smell and taste are necessary to appreciate a wine completely. Appreciate and don't abuse; take time to savour quality wine. Do not gobble it up.

Having been in the food industry for a long time, I have had the chance to work with some great sommeliers and have had some wine tasting just for myself. Wine people all have their own way of describing wines. I once met an Italian sommelier who compared wine to different types of women. Under the dim light of the closed nightclub, we had a one-to-one wine tasting. It was fun, informative, delicious and sexy. Yes, there is something sensual about wine tasting. He explained to me the different wines of Medoc (a sub-region of Bordeaux) in such a personal, unusual way that he seemed to own those vineyards and the women he was referring to. (He's Italian, after all.) He compared Saint-Estèphe to a very elegant, classy woman, Saint-Julien to a woman out and about on the town. He would change his tone, depending on which woman he was talking about, to act out the taste of wines... He would talk softly while describing a certain light, not too robust wine that would resemble a slender, blonde woman. I remember those wines because of the emotion they created, not only the beautiful taste but also the environment, the feeling, the atmosphere... The sommelier was passionate about wines, and his passion was contagious. I caught it and I sometimes even regret that nothing else but wine tasting happened on that evening! Since then, I taste, savour, take time with my wines even more and I build memories, since each wine has a different bouquet. I remember the sensation I had when trying a Macon Villages: like a piece of butter melting in my mouth! And the blackberry-blueberry taste of a Zinfandel tried for the first time in California. Or on another day, in a very appropriate place for an Italian wine tasting: in a church, I was with my friend Stéphanie who told me to smell a Barolo, saying that I would smell strawberries. Actually, it was more than that. It was like putting my nose in a strawberry jam pot that you've just opened. It was, to me, unbelievable! Or yet on another occasion, I tasted some very dry white wine, which was tart at first but when accompanied by chocolate became delicious?

NUTRITIONIST'S NOTE

The bright side of wine

An important study has proved that wine, consumed moderately each day, reduces erectile dysfunction by 30%! Perhaps this is why the French are reputed to be very good lovers?

My dad prepares a mix called *tinto de Verano* that I loved when I was a child and still do. He mixes red wine with lemonade and adds a few slices of peach. It's like a sangria but better. Wine is complex and multi-layered, not just a drink but a very special nectar you savour and enjoy. Each time you discover new tastes and sensations, it is one of our great life's pleasures! Yes, again one of them! But what a pleasure! Wines go with the season as well, and I never forget to match the food and wine with season. Choosing a bottle to accompany your dinner is a celebration in itself. Yes, we often have a bottle of wine on our dinner table. If served as an aperitif, I would always prepare something small to go with our glass. Radishes with butter and salt, prawns on skewers, hummus to add more fun and pleasure. Depending on the season, I drink white wine sometimes, but it's more according to what I eat (like a good fish in *papillote*, for example). Rosé means 'summertime' to me. It goes with the heat, the sun and the picnic on the beach. Red (and especially Bordeaux) can be too heavy when it's too hot. So rosé from May to September and red the rest of the year. It's easy. When I open a bottle of wine, I smell the cork (a technique to make sure that the wine is not corked), I pour it in a nice glass and enjoy it, sometimes on my own, on my balcony, with a cigarette, among my plants. It's one of my secret personal pleasures...

In this Covid period, while I am writing this chapter, celebration is a necessity. My friends and I are doing *apéro* video calls and when I feel particularly in a party mood, I put on a dress, makeup and high heels. I prepare some *tartines* and olives just to have a glass or two with my friends on video. Celebrating everything and anything is of huge importance!

On my blog, I wrote a chapter in 2012 about red wine and a study I read. It appears that women who prefer red wine like sex more than others.

Well, well, well... they selected 798 healthy Tuscan women and divided them into three groups. The first one for the women who drink one to two glasses of red a day, the second for those who are occasional drinkers and the third group for the ones who never drink at all. Guess what? They all completed a long survey about their sexuality before and after the study, and it appeared that the first group showed a higher score on responses related to lubrication and desire. *Et voila!* Those superpowers are accessible while having a moderate consumption and certainly according to your liver's ability to detoxify. I think I must detoxify quite well...

Rule No. 11: Never Drink Wine Without Food

Wine is a companion to our food. We never drink wine on an empty stomach. It accompanies our meals, lunches or dinners. If we order a glass of wine for an *aperitif,* each waiter, in any restaurant, always brings a glass of wine with some olives, peanuts, *saucisson, paté* and toasts or any food to prevent drinking without eating.

Drinking two bottles when there are two of us can happen. It is rare but it happened to me and my sister. We went down the street to the local *caviste* who knows his wine by heart and offered us two options of red. As we couldn't decide, we bought the two. The next morning, he wanted to know which one we drank and we said: "Both!" We didn't break our rule to go for quality. We went a bit borderline regarding our quantity rule, so we went for both. So that kind of evening happens rarely but it does; it was a long evening and we had *tartines, saucisson,* cheese and olives with wine to start with. We also had dinner, a light dinner after all that *saucisson* and cheese to balance it all out. We also drank water. That's why we felt fresh the next morning. Yes, we don't drink wine to get drunk. On the contrary, we don't get drunk when we drink our wines because they are companions to our food.

And quality over quantity even when we drink one bottle each.

Chapter Six

FOOD SHOPPING: ORGANISING THE FRENCH WAY

L ET'S BE strategic. It will take a few weeks to adapt; that's normal. Changing habits always takes a bit of time, but once figured out, it'll become natural. Being organised in your kitchen means always having a shopping list easily accessible (on your fridge, for example) so that you and your family will note what's needed. I do it, and I remember my mum writing on paper, "carrots, chicken, fresh parsley and tomatoes" and putting her notes on our fridge. Most of my friends have memories of shopping lists their mums or dads wrote.

Why don't you start showing your children the example and therefore teach them to get organised and plan ahead in the kitchen?!

Rule No. 12: Be Organised with Your Shopping and Cooking; Plan Ahead

Have a list of the basics you need to always have in your kitchen or pantry, like: olive oil, butter, nuts, brown pasta and cereals, etc. I will give you a full list in the next chapter. Make an inventory before going food shopping to make sure that you always have the basics in store. Adapt your menus according to your, and/or your family's, schedule.

Make a list of basics and a list for your weekly menus to then make the list of fresh food you will need. It doesn't take long and will be even quicker when you get used to doing it on a regular basis. I will guide you through it in the next chapter. You can also prepare some lists for the coming weeks, asking vendors on the market what will be in season soon.

Making a list will make your shopping quicker. All that will become a normality very fast; it will save you time and give you time for your coffee at the market. Going food shopping after work on the way home is the worst. After a long day, when you just want to be home as quickly as possible, it's a surefire way to end up buying everything that you don't need and spending too much money because you are tired and hungry. Then you'll find yourself facing old vegetables and other food in your fridge, ruining your appetite. Food shopping at lunch break is good (after the sacred 30-minute minimum lunch).

The ideal time for shopping for the basics and some fresh food is, to me, during the weekend. You'll still need to go once or twice during the week to refuel on fresh vegetables and fruits, your piece of meat or fresh fish. The aim is not to have anything missing or too much waste and spend more time having fun, enjoying your food, enjoying your cooking and looking after yourself. Be kind to yourself. You can also order your meat in advance at your butcher. Then you'll just have to go (on lunch break or during the weekend) and pick up your bag. Ask your fishmonger to fillet your fish and have it ready for you. Follow the season, look for variety and plan ahead. I will guide you through your planning in the next chapter. By doing this, you will eat better, feel better, prevent food waste, save money and you'll no longer ask yourself every day: "What's for dinner?"

Once the shopping is done, you can also cook your dishes in advance. If you are really busy during the week, then spend half a day at the weekend making dishes for the following two or three days. You may also freeze them. It is such a pleasure to come home from work in the evening, take your homemade dish out of the freezer, simply warm it up and enjoy! I can almost guarantee that when at work, you will already be thinking about your dinner. Once you start thinking about your evening meal and are impatient to be back home to have it, then you'll start to think like the French.

It's a very good beginning on the path of eating better and feeling better. When eating organic, very tasty food, drinking a glass of good wine and cooking become pleasures too. This half-day spent in the kitchen cooking great food at weekends can be YOUR moment. Put on music that you really like and have a glass of wine or tea, depending on the time. Find your best way to cook: your best music, your best drink... And it can change according to the season, your mood, the time of the day... On my own in my kitchen when it's raining outside, even two hours with Billie Holiday and the smell of a chocolate cake in the oven is just bliss.

Finding joy everywhere and also in my kitchen is imperative. During summertime when the barbecue season starts, my friends and/or family will prepare a huge salad together, buy nice meat at my favourite butcher's and spend hours together eating and drinking and very often making another barbecue in the evening to finish the meat left at lunch. So our barbecue time can last 12 hours!

Putting together a few leftovers and joining some friends at the last minute on the beach for an *apéro* (I told you *apéro* is a national sport in France) watching the sunset. Having a swim and having a good time is also part of my life. Find the best way to enjoy your cooking and let it become YOUR pleasure. Creating your ME time is so important.

Time + quality food + preparation = investment in health, performance and weight loss. There are only a few secrets to know. If you decide to invest some time in it every week, as for all the activities that count for you, you will make it! Simply carve out some space in your everyday routine, and a bit more time at weekends, to prepare yourself and the fuel that will nourish your cells and transform into energy. Invest in good quality food, fresh, seasonal, untreated, for life. Follow the rules from one to 12.

Your health, your ideal weight and your life challenges will be brought to a higher level. Your whole being will say 'thank you'. Are you ready to start your meal plan? That's when the magic begins.

Rule 1:   *Favour quality over quantity.*

Rule 2:   *Respect the seasons and eat seasonal food only.*

Rule 3:   *Sit down and take time to eat.*

Rule 4:   *No sodas, just drink 1.5 litres of water to hydrate.*

Rule 5:   *Balance your meals.*

Rule 6:   *Boost your self-esteem by taking care of your appearance.*

Rule 8:   *Have only three or maximum four meals a day, always seated.*

Rule 9:   *No snacking in between meals*

Rule 10: *Eat slowly and chew well.*

Rule 11: *Never drink wine without food.*

Rule 12: *Be organised with your shopping and cooking.*

Part Two

28-DAY PROGRAMME

I created this programme to make your life easier. You will find the four seasons with seven days per season. For each season, two shopping lists: one list of basics, things you should always have in your kitchen and then a list of fresh ingredients per season. For each day you will find three meals (breakfast, lunch and dinner) and for every day, some boxes that you can tick to make sure that you follow the rules of 'enough water, sport/walk, mindfulness (enjoy your food, remember?) and pleasure'. You can print this table, put it on your fridge, tick the boxes every day and be proud of yourself. That will be a very good beginning.

I divided every week in two as it won't be too much to buy at once and by going twice a week food shopping you'll make sure that you buy the freshest ingredients for your recipes. Three easy-to-execute meals a day for seven days for each season, which is 84 recipes. You may prepare some of these dishes in advance on the weekend for example. A lot of recipes can easily be made in advance, which will make your life a lot nicer... Then during the working week, when you come back home, you only have to reheat and enjoy your dinner or lunch. Or you may take your ready-made dish in a lunch box to your workplace, reheat and enjoy it. I am sure that you will make your colleagues jealous. I will tell you which dishes can be prepared in advance, but almost all of them can.

You may also choose to cook more food than you need in advance and freeze what is left. Freezing is not bad at all, as it maintains all the nutrients and vitamins. It is so good to come home knowing that you have homemade, ready-to-defrost dishes.

Make soups. Simply heated and topped with grated cheese, a soup can make miracles. Don't waste. Reuse, check the dates and if you can't use ingredients straight away, put them in the freezer.

Variety and good-quality food are my mojo. I am sure that you too can enjoy French-style healthy cuisine. It's just a question of organisation and changing your habits a little to become a bit French yourself.

Enjoy!

The Basics

Here is the list of basics that you should always have at home throughout the year. You should buy these ingredients once a week or every two weeks to keep your kitchen shelves and cupboards stocked.

List of basics:

- Olive oil
- Vegetable oil
- Truffle oil
- Butter
- Nuts (almonds, walnuts and hazelnuts)
- Brown pasta/rice
- Cereals (oat flakes, cornflakes)
- Tomato coulis
- Quinoa
- Flour
- Salt/pepper
- Eggs
- Milk
- Brown onions
- Garlic
- Green tea
- Honey
- Agave syrup
- Simple but good red wine for cooking (Pinot Noir, Merlot)
- Red wine for drinking (according to your taste)
- Beef, chicken and/or vegetable bouillon/stock cubes
- Homemade or good-quality jam
- Coffee
- Sugar
- Dijon mustard
- Dried herbs (oregano, thyme, *herbes de Provence*, rosemary, *bouquet garni*)
- Spices: paprika, turmeric, cumin
- Tins of chickpeas
- Coconut flakes
- Dried fruits (apricots, prunes, dates)
- Tins of tuna in brine
- Tins of tomatoes in juice
- Tins of anchovies
- Tomato paste
- Baking powder
- Cocoa powder
- Baking paper

I love each season for different reasons, and I have my favourite flavours and perfumes in each of them. I am sure you will find yours! Let's start with spring!

SPRING

Day	Breakfast	Lunch	Dinner	Well-being
1	Black coffee, marbled cake	Seabream fillet in *papillotte*, tomato and asparagus	Pea soup, parmesan cheese *tuiles*, avocado vinaigrette	☐ water ☐ sport/walk ☐ mindfulness ☐ pleasure
2	Green tea, baguette and banana	Bread-crumbed veal escalopes, potato *écrasé*	Spring courgettes *gratin* and melon and basil gazpacho	☐ water ☐ sport/walk ☐ mindfulness ☐ pleasure
3	Black coffee, oatmeal, coconut flakes, dried fruits, nuts, agave syrup	Ratatouille with scrambled eggs	Niçoise salad	☐ water ☐ sport/walk ☐ mindfulness ☐ pleasure
4	Green tea, brown bread toast, butter and jam	Salmon and green apple tartare with sautéed green beans	Red pepper stuffed with quinoa	☐ water ☐ sport/walk ☐ mindfulness ☐ pleasure
5	Black coffee, croissant or *pain au chocolat*	Cod aioli	Cherry tomato *clafoutis*, black olives and thyme	☐ water ☐ sport/walk ☐ mindfulness ☐ pleasure
6	Black coffee, oatmeal, coconut flakes, dried fruits, nuts and agave syrup	Beef *carpaccio* with olive paste on toast and rocket and herb salad	Cold pesto pasta salad	☐ water ☐ sport/walk ☐ mindfulness ☐ pleasure
7	Smoked salmon, fresh spinach, brown toast, butter, black coffee	Prawns with pastis sauce fennel and rice	Grilled asparagus, goat cheese, soft boiled eggs, green leaves, lemon zest and truffle oil	☐ water ☐ sport/walk ☐ mindfulness ☐ pleasure

On Friday evening or Saturday morning, make your list for the basics you need and the fresh food for days one, two, three and four. Go shopping either on Saturday or Sunday morning, depending on when you are planning to cook.

For your week ahead, dishes you may prepare in advance:

For Day One, you can prepare the marbled cake. (It will stay fresh for a few days.) The pea soup can be prepared in advance (without the *tuile*) and the vinaigrette can be made too. It will last a week in the fridge, as it's covered with oil, so I would even prepare a big bowl of vinaigrette for the whole week and use when needed.

For Day Two, you can boil the eggs for breakfast in advance and make your breadcrumbs (if you make your own). The courgette and onions for dinner can also be fried. You'll just have to assemble the *gratin* on the day. The *gazpacho* can be made in advance. Just leave it out of the fridge for at least half an hour before having it. It's even nicer.

For Day Three, the *ratatouille* can be made in advance and will be even more delicious reheated.

For Day Four, you can definitely cook the quinoa even a few days in advance.

NUTRITIONIST'S NOTE

The power of herbs and spices

It is impossible to separate the art of French cooking from the wonderful heritage of its aromatic herbs.

Although they have been used for centuries, herbs still play a very important role in the refined dishes of modern French cuisine. Their superpower? Spreading the magic of their phototherapeutic molecules under the guise of scenting our plates and taking us on incredible gourmet journeys. You will find notes about the qualities of our herbs next to Marlene's recipes.

Shopping List for Days One, Two, Three and Four, for 2 people

- 2 seabream fillets of around 180g each
- 4 tomatoes
- ½ bunch of spring onion
- ½ medium potato
- 400g fresh peas in a pod (these will give you half the weight once out of the pod)
- 2 tbsp fresh mint chopped
- 2 to 3 lemons
- 390g parmesan cheese
- 1 avocado
- 200g breadcrumbs or old bread
- 2 x 180g veal escalope
- 300g new potatoes
- 400g pale green spring courgettes
- 200ml liquid cream
- Half of an orange melon
- 2 cucumbers
- 1 courgette
- 2 red bell peppers
- 1eggplant
- A bouquet of fresh basil
- 5 broad bean pods
- 1 red bell pepper
- 2 sprigs of celery
- 1 tbsp of small *Niçoise* black olives
- 2 purple artichoke hearts
- 6 radishes
- Brown bread
- 2 salmon fillets
- ½ green apple
- A quarter of a pomegranate
- Chives
- 400g green beans
- 260g feta cheese

Basics from Your Pantry

- ½ garlic clove, crushed
- 400ml vegetable stock cube
- Small pinch of caster sugar
- 17 fresh eggs
- Red wine vinegar
- Salt and pepper
- Butter
- 1½ brown onions
- Olive oil
- 2 tbsp of oats
- Dried fruits
- 1 tbsp of coconut flakes
- 4 anchovies from a tin
- 1 small tin of tuna in brine
- Homemade jam
- 100g quinoa
- Half a tsp smoked paprika
- Half a tsp turmeric
- Half a tsp ground cumin

Breakfast: Black coffee, marbled cake
Lunch: Seabream fillet in *papillotte*, tomato and asparagus
Dinner: Pea soup, parmesan cheese *tuiles*, avocado vinaigrette

BREAKFAST

For the vanilla part of the cake:
30g butter
5 egg yolks
200g sugar
70g liquid cream
100g flour
2g baking powder
1 vanilla pod

For the chocolate part:
30g butter
4 egg yolks
110g sugar
20g cocoa powder
2g baking powder
90g flour
60g liquid cream

The marbled cake is made up of one vanilla section and one chocolate section, which are combined to create a 'marbled' effect before baking.

For the vanilla section, melt the butter. Mix the egg yolks (keep the whites to make a white omelette, light and full of proteins) with the sugar in a food processor or with a whisk by hand for a few minutes. Then add the cream to your yolks followed by the flour and baking powder and mix gently. Add the butter and the vanilla pod that you will have to cut in half lengthwise, taking out and keeping the inside for your cake. Keep aside.

Do the same for the chocolate part. Melt the butter. Mix the sugar with egg yolks and cocoa powder. Add the cream, flour and baking powder. Whisk gently and add the butter.

Preheat the oven to 165°C. Butter and flour the baking tin. Garnish one-quarter of the tin with the plain cake mix, a second quarter with the chocolate mix, then the half left with the plain mix. Then marble the cake; stick a spatula into it a few times at different places on the cake to create a marbling effect. Put in the oven for 45 minutes. Let it cool down before taking it out of its tin.

LUNCH

2 seabream fillets of around 180g each
2 tomatoes
2 asparagus

1 lemon
Baking paper
Olive oil
Salt and pepper

Preheat the oven to 180°C. Cut two sheets of baking paper around 40cm long. Place one fillet of fish on each sheet, and add one sliced tomato and one sliced asparagus per fish. Add salt and pepper, squeeze some lemon juice on them and add a splash of olive oil. Close the parcel making a hem with the two edges of paper lengthwise and close the other edges by rolling them like a *bonbon*. Cook for 25 minutes.

DINNER

½ bunch of spring onion
1 medium potato
½ garlic clove, crushed
400ml vegetable stock cube
400g fresh peas in a pod (you will have half the weight once removed from the pods.)
2 tbsp fresh mint chopped

Salt and pepper
Small pinch of caster sugar
½ tbsp fresh lemon or lime juice
1 tsp mustard
Olive oil
Red wine vinegar
Salt and pepper
One sheet of baking paper

Boil some salted water, and boil two or three tbsp of peas for two minutes before putting them in a bowl with ice cubes to stop the cooking process. They will be the decoration for your soup.

Preheat the oven to 180°C. Peel the potato, dice it and roughly chop the spring onions. Bring 400ml of water to the boil, then add the vegetable cube and mix so that the cube dissolves. Cook your potato and spring onions in the stock for 15 minutes. When you reach 10 minutes and the potatoes are soft, add the peas and cook them too for the last five minutes. We don't want to boil them for too long so as not to lose the taste and the vitamins.

Meanwhile, grate the parmesan cheese and make some heaps of around 10cm diameter (and not too flat, not too thick) on the baking paper and bake them for 10 minutes until the cheese melts and becomes golden brown. When cooked, let them cool down and take them off the paper.

Cut the avocado in half. Take out the stone. Make your vinaigrette by adding the mustard, olive oil, vinegar and salt and pepper to a small bowl. Mix and pour a table spoon onto each half of the avocado. When the 15 minutes are done for the peas, blend the peas, potato and spring onion and serve straight away or wait until it's cold. Sprinkle the peas that you kept for decoration and the parmesan cheese *tuile* on the top. Enjoy the avocado just like that (either cut in half, or peeled and sliced) with the vinaigrette.

Breakfast: Green tea, baguette toast, butter and jam and banana
Lunch: Bread-crumbed veal escalopes, potato *écrasé*
Dinner: Spring courgettes *gratin* with melon and gazpacho

BREAKFAST

Brown bread toast
Butter and homemade or good-
quality jam

Black coffee
Banana

LUNCH

200g breadcrumbs or old bread if
you make your own
2 x 180g veal escalope
300g new potatoes
2 knobs of butter

1 egg
A few sprigs of parsley roughly
chopped
Salt and pepper
Vegetable oil

Ecrasé potato is a very quick mashed potato, as it's made with a fork;
the aim is to have nice chunks of potatoes.

Boil some water with two big pinches of salt. Peel the potatoes and cut them into four or six cubes each according to their size. When the water is boiling, put the potatoes in for around 15 minutes (until they are soft).

Take two soup plates, crack the egg in one with salt and pepper and put the breadcrumbs in the other with salt and pepper too. If you use your old bread, blitz it in a food processor to make some crumbs that you can store for later dishes. (The bread has to be very old and hard; otherwise, the blade will stay stuck into your bread). Heat a splash of oil with a knob of butter in a frying pan. Dip each escalope first in the egg, then in the breadcrumbs and then cook them in the pan for around four minutes on each side.

Meanwhile, drain the potatoes and mash them roughly with a fork before adding salt and pepper and a knob of butter. Finish with the parsley on the top.

DINNER

400g pale green spring courgettes	Half a melon
1 and a half brown onions	1 cucumber
1 egg	A few leaves of fresh basil
200ml liquid cream	Olive oil
	50g parmesan cheese
	Salt and pepper

Slice the onion, wash the courgettes and dice them into cubes of 1cm. Heat some olive oil in a pan and cook the onions and courgettes on medium heat for 20 minutes with salt and pepper. Preheat the oven to 180°C. While they are cooking, crack the egg in a bowl, pour the cream on it and mix with a fork with salt and pepper. When the courgettes and onions are cooked, put them in the cream and mix gently. Put them on a baking tray for two. Grate your parmesan on top and cook in the oven for 15 minutes.

NUTRITIONIST'S NOTE

Basil

More than 150 varieties of basil have found their way onto our plates. Roman Basil or *Pistou* (as it is called in Provence) is best when in salads, soups or mixed with raw vegetables, which it also disinfects. In other areas, it calms gastric spasms and heals intestinal infections.

Breakfast: Oatmeal, coconut flakes, dried and
fresh fruits, nuts and agave syrup
Lunch: Ratatouille with scrambled eggs
Dinner: Niçoise salad

BREAKFAST

Black coffee
2 tbsp of oats
1 tbsp of coconut flakes

Dried fruit and nuts of your choice
Agave syrup or honey to your taste

LUNCH

1 courgette
1 red bell pepper
1 aubergine
A few leaves of fresh basil

4 eggs
Olive oil
Salt and pepper

Wash all the vegetables and dice the courgette into 1cm cubes. Dice
the red pepper and the aubergine with the skin – the same way as the
courgette. Heat the olive oil and cook the vegetables half-covered by a
lid for around half an hour on low heat, then add salt and pepper. If it's
too dry and not cooked enough, add a bit of water. The vegetables have
to be nearly melting. When they're ready, add the fresh basil on the top.

At the last minute, crack your eggs in a bowl and whisk with salt
and pepper. Cook the eggs with a bit of oil in a frying pan and mix
continuously for two to three minutes (depending on if you like them a
bit runny or not) with a wooden spoon to scramble them.

Like the tomato sauce and different gratins, the *ratatouille* is
wonderful reheated, even reheated a few times.

DINNER

2 ripe tomatoes
5 broad bean pods
1 red bell pepper
Half a cucumber
2 hard-boiled eggs
2 sprigs of celery

1 tbsp of small *Niçoise* black olives
2 purple artichoke hearts
4 anchovies
6 radishes
1 small tin of tuna in brine
A few leaves of fresh basil

4 tbsp olive oil   A pinch of salt and pepper
1 tbsp red wine vinegar

Wash all your vegetables, peel the cucumber and slice it very finely. Take the broad beans out of their pods. For the purple artichokes, take off the outer leaves (half of the artichoke) until you reach the tender part. Cut them in half and slice them very finely. (If you do that in advance, plunge them in water with a squeeze of lemon; otherwise, they will get dark.)

Slice the tomatoes, radishes, celery and peppers, and shell the eggs before cutting them into quarters. In a nice salad bowl, plate all the vegetables first, then the tuna on the top with olives, anchovies and basil. Prepare your dressing by mixing five tbsp of olive oil, two tbsp of vinegar and salt and pepper, or reuse the vinaigrette made for Day One if you still have some in your fridge and enjoy!

Breakfast: Green tea, brown bread toast, butter and jam
Lunch: Salmon and green apple tartare with sautéed green beans
Dinner: Red pepper stuffed with quinoa

BREAKFAST

Green tea

Brown bread, toasted

Butter

Homemade or good-quality jam

LUNCH

2 salmon fillets, no skin (your fishmonger can do this)

½ a green apple

¼ a pomegranate

Chives

Lemon

Black pepper

Dice the salmon into quite small cubes (1cm max). Keep the skin on the apple (for extra colour and vitamins) and dice into very, very little cubes (smaller than the salmon). While preparing the rest, put your apple dices in a bowl with cold water and lemon to avoid oxidation.

Take the seeds out of the pomegranate and chop the chives very finely. Mix the salmon with apple, pomegranate and chives gently. Season with black pepper and lemon according to your taste.

This is why it's so important to buy organic produce. Apples keep most of their vitamins in their skin, and when buying organic, you just have to rinse them instead of peeling them.

DINNER

½ brown onion

A few leaves of parsley

1 red pepper

100g feta cheese

100g quinoa

Salt and pepper

Olive oil

Slice the onion finely, heat the olive oil in a frying pan and cook it on medium till it becomes brown and translucent. Boil 500ml of water.

When the onion is cooked, add the quinoa in the pan. Cover the quinoa with hot water, add salt and pepper and let it simmer for around 20 minutes, stirring from time to time and adding a bit more water if it becomes dry but is not yet cooked. The quinoa has to be cooked and dry with no water left in the pan. That's why it's important to stay around and add some water little by little.

Meanwhile, preheat the oven at 180°C. Wash the red pepper, cut it in half and take off the seeds. Cut the feta into cubes of 1cm, chop the parsley roughly and keep a few leaves for decoration. When the quinoa is cooked, mix it with the parsley and feta cheese. Then put the mix on each part of the red bell pepper and place them on a baking tray for around 20 minutes, until the red pepper is soft. Sprinkle the parsley leaves on the top for decoration.

Before Day Five, always check your list of basics and go shopping again on your lunch break on Day Three or Day Four for the rest of the week. You may prepare some dishes in advance – in the evenings or mornings – depending on whether you are an early bird or not.

Dishes you can prepare in advance:

For Day Five, you can prepare the *aioli* sauce in advance.

For Day Six, you can prepare the olive paste for the beef *carpaccio* and the pesto for the *pesto* pasta salad.

Shopping List for Days Five, Six and Seven for two people

- 400g cod
- 2 carrots
- 2 small potatoes
- 1 courgette
- 100g green beans
- 1 lemon
- 120g parmesan cheese
- 300g cherry tomatoes
- 100g pitted black olives
- 2.5 tbsp of fresh thyme leaves
- 175ml milk
- 400g beef *carpaccio* (to be made by your butcher)
- Half of a red onion
- A few capers
- A few croutons or slices of old bread
- Rocket salad
- 300g raw prawns
- ¼ tsp chilli flakes or powder
- 2 small fennels washed and cut into fine 5mm slices
- 100ml *pastis*
- 10g fresh tarragon roughly chiselled
- 100g feta cheese
- 150g green asparagus
- 50g fresh goat cheese

Basics from your pantry

- Vegetable oil
- 3 garlic cloves
- 1 tsp Dijon mustard
- 6 eggs
- 65g flour
- Olive oil
- Butter
- 250g pasta (either *penne* or *farfalle*)
- ½ tsp dry oregano
- 75ml vegetable *bouillon*/stock cubes
- A pinch of paprika
- 300g rice
- Truffle oil

Breakfast: Black coffee, croissant or *pain au chocolat*
Lunch: Cod aioli
Dinner: Cherry tomato *clafoutis*

BREAKFAST

Black coffee   Croissant or *pain au chocolat*

LUNCH

400g cod   100g green beans
2 carrots   Vegetable oil
2 small potatoes   3 garlic cloves
1 courgette   1 tsp Dijon mustard
2 eggs   1 lemon
                                      Salt and pepper

The *aioli* is part of *Provençal* heritage and is traditionally a garlicky sauce, prepared with a pestle and mortar (my grandmother used to make it this way) and made only with a garlic emulsion and olive oil. With time, it evolved and many chefs, myself included, now make a variant of *aioli*, which is a mayonnaise with garlic. It's very easy, and in this recipe, you will learn how to make a homemade mayonnaise (wonderful with meat, fish and vegetables) and by adding some garlic, you'll obtain the *aioli* that we make in my family. Two recipes in one!

Peel the carrots and potatoes and rinse them with the green beans and courgette. In a small pot, bring some water to the boil, and when it's boiling, plunge the eggs gently and boil them for nine minutes. If you have a steamer, it's better to cook the vegetables in it to keep all the vitamins. If not, boil some water in a pot, add a big pinch of salt, cut the potatoes into four or six cubes (depending on the size) and when it's boiling, add the courgette, carrots and potatoes and boil them for around 10 minutes.

Boil or steam the green beans in a different pot with a big pinch of salt as they need less time to cook and they have to stay a bit crunchy

Do the same for the cod. Boil some water with salt and cook the cod in water. Putting cold fish in the hot water will stop that water from boiling for a while but when it starts boiling again, stop the heat, cover and let the fish cook slowly for 10 minutes. If you use a steamer, the time is nearly the same as the water-cooking process; leave the cod and courgette for 10 minutes. Then leave the carrots and potatoes for five more minutes, as they take longer to cook.

Whilst everything is cooking, make your *aioli* sauce:

Peel and cut the garlic very finely in a small bowl that you will place on a folded kitchen cloth (to stop the bowl moving, as your two hands will be busy). Put in one tsp mustard, add the egg yolk and stir. Then, in one hand, take the bottle of oil and in the other hand, an electric whisk (if you don't have one, you can use a manual one; it's good for the arms). Very slowly, pour the oil on the mustard and yolk mix while whisking.

It has to be just a small drizzle of oil continuously without stopping whisking until the mix becomes thick; you will notice that the consistency changes. The more oil you add, the more *aioli* you will have. When it's done, add the salt and pepper and a drizzle of lemon juice.

Then, add the garlic a little at a time and not all three cloves at once, as it may be too strong. Put a bit of garlic in and taste. Then add some more if you like it strong and garlicky like me.

Shell the eggs, cut them in half and, in a nice round or oval plate, place the cod and then the vegetables and eggs. Put the *aioli* in a nice little bowl and place it on the big plate next to the fish and vegetables.

NUTRITIONIST'S NOTE

Thyme

This is one of the most widely used plants since ancient Egypt and ancient Greece and was recommended by Hippocrates, the father of medicine himself. What an impressive record!

It is easier to understand its long-running appeal when you know that it is a proven bactericide. In cooking, it is added to Mediterranean dishes, largely for its aromatic scent and also to stimulate our appetite, cleanse our intestine and promote healthy digestion.

One small thyme tea in the morning will have the same effect.

DINNER

300g cherry tomatoes	1 egg
100g pitted black olives	25cl olive oil
2.5 tbsp of thyme leaves	40g parmesan cheese
60g flour + 5g for the tin	Black pepper
175ml milk	A knob of butter for the tin

Preheat the oven to 180°C. Butter a baking tin for two and then sprinkle flour in it. Chop the olives roughly and mix them in a bowl with the thyme leaves.

In another bowl, whisk the egg with the flour and pepper. Add the milk, the parmesan cheese grated and the olive oil without stopping whisking. Wash the tomatoes, spread them first in your baking tin and then spread the olives on the top. Pour the egg and parmesan mix on the top and cook for 15 to 20 minutes. Eat warm or cold.

Breakfast: Oatmeal, coconut flakes, dried fruits, nuts and agave syrup

Lunch: Beef carpaccio with black olive paste
on toast, rocket and herb salad

Dinner: Cold pesto pasta salad

BREAKFAST

2 tbsp of oats
1 tbsp of coconut flakes
Dried fruit and nuts of your choice

Agave syrup or honey to your taste
Milk

Heat up the milk. When warm, turn off the heat and add the oats. Leave it to rest on the side while you slice the banana. Add the honey and slices of banana and eat warm.

LUNCH

400g beef *carpaccio* (to be made by your butcher)
½ red onion
A few capers
50g parmesan cheese

Olive oil
50g pitted black olives
A few croutons or slices of old bread
Rocket salad, a big bunch of parsley

Slice the red onion very finely and cut the parmesan with a potato peeler to make some fine shavings.

Put the olives in a food processor with a bit of olive oil to make the paste.

Toast the bread, and meanwhile, spread the beef slices on a plate. Sprinkle the onion slices on the beef, then the capers, parmesan and a few leaves of parsley finely chopped. Finish with a drizzle of olive oil.

Spread the olive paste on your toast and serve the *carpaccio* with rocket salad, roughly chopped parsley and olive paste toast.

DINNER

250g pasta (either penne or farfalle)
50g feta cheese
50g cherry tomatoes
30g parmesan cheese

For the *pesto*:
1 garlic clove
1 bunch of basil
Olive oil

Boil some water in a medium pan with a big pinch of salt. Cook the pasta for 15 minutes or according to the instructions on the pack. Meanwhile, wash the cherry tomatoes, cut the feta into cubes and make your *pesto*: wash the basil and peel the garlic. Put them in a small food processor. Sprinkle with salt and pepper and a good splash of olive oil. If too thick, add a bit of oil. When the pasta is cooked, add the *pesto* first and mix well for it to coat the pasta, then the feta cheese and cherry tomatoes. Finish with some olive oil and grated parmesan cheese. To eat either warm or cold.

Breakfast: Baby spinach, smoked salmon,
toast, butter, jam and black coffee
Lunch: Prawns with pastis sauce, fennel and rice
Dinner: Grilled asparagus, goat cheese, soft boiled
eggs, green leaves, lemon zest and truffle oil

BREAKFAST

200g baby spinach
Butter
Vegetable oil
200g smoked salmon

Brown bread toasted
Slice of lemon
Black pepper

Heat a pan with a knob of butter and a bit of oil. On a medium heat, quickly fry the baby spinach but not too much – to keep the vitamins. On your toast, put some butter and smoked salmon and finish with a squeeze of lemon and black pepper.

LUNCH

300g raw prawns
½ tbsp of dry thyme leaves
1 garlic clove crushed
Zest of half a lemon
50ml olive oil
60g feta cheese
¼ tsp chilli flakes or powder
½ tsp dry oregano
2 small fennels washed and cut
into fine slices of 5mm

100ml *pastis*
75ml vegetable bouillon
35g butter
10g fresh tarragon roughly
chiselled
Salt and pepper
A pinch of paprika
300g rice

Pastis is a typical anise-flavoured drink from Marseille in the south of France.

Put all the prawns in a bowl with the olive oil, thyme and lemon zests. Mix well, cover and leave it in the fridge for at least one hour (ideally overnight). In another bowl, put the feta into cubes with one tablespoon of olive oil, hot pepper and oregano. Mix, cover and put in the fridge. (This can be prepared the day before like the prawns.)

Heat some olive oil in a pan on high heat and grill the prawns for one minute on each side. Keep them on the side and in the same pan cook the fennel for around 10 minutes on medium heat till it becomes brown and a bit tender.

Meanwhile, boil some water with salt and cook the rice. Pour the *pastis* onto the fennel. Cook for one minute. Add the bouillon. Cook again for two to three minutes. The liquid needs to be reduced by two-thirds. Lower the heat, add the tarragon and half tsp salt, a bit of black pepper and then add the butter and the prawns with the marinade. Mix gently for two minutes to obtain a silky sauce and finish the cooking of the prawns. Serve the rice, the prawns and fennel on the side and *feta* on the top. Finish with a bit of paprika and a drizzle of olive oil. It's wonderful!

DINNER

1 bunch of green asparagus	Zest of half a lemon
2 eggs	A few drops of truffle oil
50g soft goat cheese	Olive oil
Two handfuls of green leaves (lettuce or rocket)	Salt and pepper

Wash and cut off the hard end of the asparagus (not too much so as not to waste; it would be such a shame). I cut around one centimetre off the hard end. Then I peel (with a potato peeler) the hardest part on half of the asparagus lengthwise. It will make the hard part tender and allow the heat to reach the middle of this part quicker. Wash your green leaves.

Heat a frying pan with a bit of olive oil. Grill the asparagus on medium heat with salt and pepper. Meanwhile, boil some water and plunge the eggs in gently for six minutes. When cooked, submerge them in cold water to stop the cooking process and shell them gently (as they are soft and runny inside).

When the asparagus stalks are soft and grilled, place them on the green leaves on a plate. Add the eggs cut in half, the crumbled goat's cheese, the lemon zest and a few drops of truffle oil.

Light digestion after a great meal

A good meal can be divine, and it is only natural to let oneself be carried away by the flavours, from the starter all the way to the dessert. But some organs, once the enthusiasm of greed has passed, will start to produce pretty uncomfortable sensations. Fortunately, there are natural remedies that are very effective in facilitating the work of digestion, keeping you feeling light and happy.

Lemon: Despite its acidic taste, lemon is actually alkalising once in the digestive system. It is very beneficial for the liver, stimulating the production of bile, which is essential for the digestion of fats. The juice from half an organic lemon with a little warm water is a quick and beneficial mini-detox.

Cider Vinegar: A real cure-all in natural medicine and particularly useful for solving digestive issues. Its secret? Acetic acid, which is full of beneficial properties.

To benefit from its superpowers, you must choose an organic, unpasteurised cider vinegar that has been aged for at least 10 years. It has a proven beneficial effect on blood sugar levels, particularly after a meal rich in sugars. To make your digestion lighter and easier, take two tablespoons of cider vinegar with a glass of hot water before the meal.

Hot water bottles: Who would believe that this grandmotherly object can help digestion? The liver knows perfectly well! Once we know that the liver is the purification centre of the body and that its optimal temperature is 39 to 41 degrees Celsius, the hot water bottle then becomes a very natural choice.

Why does it work? Because a hot water bottle, placed on the liver (on the right hypochondria), will raise its temperature to 42 degrees, causing a small artificial fever. This heat destroys pathogens and toxins. It is ideal after a good meal as well as during the heavy festive season.

Rosemary Herbal Tea: Rosemary is THE essential herb for easy digestion and to maintain the healthiest of digestive systems! A simple bag of organic tea or an infusion of a few twigs will work wonders in a few minutes.

SUMMER

Day	Breakfast	Lunch	Dinner	Well-being
1	Fresh fruit salad, coffee, bread, butter and jam	Round summer courgettes stuffed with goat cheese, couscous salad	Heirloom tomato tart with grilled chickpea salad	☐ water ☐ sport/walk ☐ mindfulness ☐ pleasure
2	Fresh fruit salad, black coffee and croissant	Seabass fillets in *papillotte* with lime, rice, broad bean and pea salad	Spanish tortilla, grilled chorizo and red pepper salad	☐ water ☐ sport/walk ☐ mindfulness ☐ pleasure
3	Green tea, bread, butter and jam	Veal saltimbocca, warm green bean salad	Plate *fraîcheur*, burrata, water-melon, melon, Parma ham, rocket salad, black olive tapenade	☐ water ☐ sport/walk ☐ mindfulness ☐ pleasure
4	Black coffee, oat meal with coconut flakes and fresh peach	Summer braised chicken with tomato and polenta	Courgette flan, quinoa, prawns and cucumber salad	☐ water ☐ sport/walk ☐ mindfulness ☐ pleasure
5	Green tea, 2 poached eggs, yoghurt with fresh blueberries	Salmon mi-cuit, pink hummus and lemon fresh peas	Rocket salad with fresh apricots, roasted hazelnuts, feta and tomato chutney on toast	☐ water ☐ sport/walk ☐ mindfulness ☐ pleasure
6	Green tea, smoked salmon and butter on brown bread	Vegetarian lasagna with green salad	Caponata on toast with marinated beef skewers	☐ water ☐ sport/walk ☐ mindfulness ☐ pleasure
7	Black coffee, fried eggs and baguette	*Cordons bleus*, heirloom tomato salad	Arancini with tomato sauce and green leaves	☐ water ☐ sport/walk ☐ mindfulness ☐ pleasure

For your week ahead, dishes you may prepare in advance:

For Day One, The fruit salad can be made in bigger quantities so you have some for a few days; a squeeze of lemon juice on it will give a nice kick but also avoid the oxidation that turns the fruits brown. The stuffed courgettes can be made one or two days in advance. For the tomato tart for dinner, if you make your own pastry you can prepare this even a few days in advance, you can also double or triple the proportions and freeze the dough in cling film and keep for every time you fancy a quiche or a tart...

For Day Two, the *papillotte* with the seabass can be prepared the day before, as well as the rice for the salad. For the peas, you can do half cooked and half raw (it's delicious) and will give a nice crunch to your salad.

For Day Three, the veal saltimbocca (this can be replaced by chicken breast) can also be prepared a day or two before

For Day Four, the chicken can be pan-fried in advance; you'll just have to put the last ingredients together. The courgette flan for the evening can be made in advance too, if you don't have time to make the flan, you can at least cook the courgettes, keep them in the fridge for a few days and make your flan last minute.

Shopping List for Days One, Two, Three and Four for two people

- 2 peaches
- 2 fresh apricots
- A few berries (blueberries or blackberries)
- Coconut flakes
- Half of a lemon
- 4 or 6 round green courgettes (depending on the size)
- 1 Fresh goat cheese of 150g
- Any green leaves
- 1 ready to roll puff pastry
- 100g ripe heirloom tomatoes
- 100g cheddar cheese
- 200g couscous
- Sprigs of parsley and coriander
- 1 lemon (juice and zests)
- Lettuce leaves
- 2 seabass fillets of 180g each
- 1 lime
- 50g fresh peas
- 50g fresh broad beans
- 300g potatoes
- 50g hot or soft chorizo
- 2 red bell peppers
- 1 garlic clove
- Rocket or lettuce salad leaves
- 2 escalope veal (or chicken) of 180g each

- 4 slices of Parma ham
- A few sage leaves (optional but very nice)
- Half a glass of either Madeira wine or Port wine
- 400g fresh green beans
- 1 Burrata
- Half of a small watermelon
- Half of a melon
- 2 slices of Parma ham
- 200g rocket leaves
- 200g black olives pitted
- 50g capers in brine
- 2 shallots
- 2 chicken legs
- 150ml chicken stock

- 1 garlic clove
- A few sprigs of fresh thyme
- 200g cherry tomato
- 2 plum tomatoes quartered
- 200g can cannellini beans
- ½ of a green chilli finely sliced
- 85g fine grain polenta
- 40g parmesan grated
- Small bunch of basil
- 5 long courgettes
- 250ml liquid *crème fraîche*
- 150g raw prawns
- ¼ of cucumber halved and sliced
- 50g lettuce leaves
- 1 baguette

Basics from your pantry

- Green tea
- Oat meal
- Milk
- 200g rice
- 1 tbsp of Dijon mustard
- 5 onions
- 50g hazelnuts
- 200g Chickpeas
- 60g quinoa
- 8 eggs
- Knob of butter
- 2 or 3 anchovies

Day One

Breakfast: Fresh fruit salad, coffee, bread, butter and jam
Lunch: Round summer courgettes stuffed
with goat cheese, couscous salad
Dinner: Heirloom tomato tart with grilled chickpea salad

BREAKFAST

1 peach

1 apricot

A few berries

Squeeze of one lemon

Cut the peach and apricot into cubes or fine slices. Add the squeeze of the lemon and the berries.

LUNCH

4/6 summer round courgettes
(depending on the size)

150g fresh goat cheese

1 onion

A few sprigs of parsley and
coriander

Olive or vegetable oil

50g crushed hazelnuts

1 lemon (zest and juice)

A few leaves of lettuce

Salt and pepper

200g couscous

Boil 1 litre of water with a tsp salt, rinse the courgettes and plunge them in the water for 15 minutes (till they are a little soft); you can also steam them. If you boil them, keep the hot water, put your couscous in a salad bowl or baking tray, cover with hot water to the top, add a bit of olive oil, cover and let the grain absorb the water.

Cut off the 'hat' of the courgettes and scoop the inside flesh of the courgettes with a tea spoon, then set aside. Chop the parsley and coriander finely and crush the hazelnuts. Preheat the oven at 180°C. Slice the onion finely and cook slowly in a pan with a bit of oil till they are tender and add the courgettes flesh to them with salt and pepper. When the courgettes and onion mix is soft, let it to cool down for a few minutes and add the goat cheese, half of the parsley and hazelnuts.

Put this mix into each courgette and close them with their 'hat'.

Cook them in the oven for 15 minutes (until they are really soft and start to be golden. Meanwhile, check the couscous; if it's still hard, add a bit of hot water on the top till the water is absorbed. Zest the lemon and squeeze it. When the couscous is ready add the herbs and lemon juice and zest. Adjust the seasoning according to your taste and enjoy!

DINNER

100g ripe heirloom tomatoes
100g cheddar cheese
1 tbsp of mustard
1 ready to roll short-crust pastry
Salt and pepper

Olive oil and a few leaves of basil
for decoration
200g chickpeas
Zests and juice of 1 lemon

Preheat the oven at 180°C. Put your dough in a mould and pick the bottom with a fork. Spread the mustard on it.

Slice the tomatoes and cut the cheddar cheese into fine pieces. Spread the cheese nicely on the mustard then the tomatoes. Add salt and pepper. and cook for 25 min. Put the chickpeas in a pan with a bit of oil and cook them till they are a bit brown and become crispy. Zest and juice the lemon and add it to the hot chickpeas. When the tart is ready, add a drizzle of olive oil and the basil leaves chopped on the top. Eat with the warm or cold chickpea salad.

Breakfast: Fresh fruit salad, black coffee and croissant
Lunch: Seabass fillets in *papillotte* with lime,
rice, broad bean and pea salad
Dinner: Spanish tortilla, grilled chorizo and red bell pepper salad

BREAKFAST

Make the same fresh fruit salad as Day One, add a croissant and black coffee for the French touch and if you are very hungry.

LUNCH

2 fillets of seabass of 180g each
1 lime
50g fresh peas
50g broad beans

200 of rice
A few sprigs of parsley
Baking paper

Cook the rice in boiling and salted water. If the peas are not cooked in advance, cook them in a small saucepan with boiling water and salt for 10 minutes, then plunge them in a salad bowl full of ice cubes. They will keep their beautiful colour.

Preheat the oven at 180°C.

On a baking tray, spread two baking sheets, put one fish fillet per sheet, season with salt and pepper, a squeeze of lime and close the paper like a 'bonbon', so as not to have any air coming into the *papillotte*. Put the fish in the oven for 15/20 min, not too much as seabass is a delicate fish and to eat it dry would be a crime. While the rice and fish are cooking, take the broad beans out of the pod. When ready add the beans and peas to the rice, season with salt, pepper, olive oil and lime juice.

DINNER

300g new or Yukon potatoes	1 garlic clove
50g chorizo (hot or soft)	6 eggs
2 onions	Rocket or lettuce salad leaves
2 red bell peppers	Vegetable oil

Peel and cut the potatoes into cubes, peel and slice the onions. In a frying pan put quite a lot of oil (that's the secret of having a very moist tortilla), cook your potatoes and onions on low heat, add salt and pepper and let it cook till the potatoes are tender.

Meanwhile, crack the eggs in a bowl and add salt and pepper, whisk.

When the potatoes are cooked, put them in the eggs, mix, add some more oil in the same pan (where you cooked the potatoes) and pour in the eggs and potatoes mix.

Fry on a slow heat, otherwise the bottom might burn.

Wash and remove the seeds of the red pepper and cut it in long slices. Cook them in a small pan with olive oil. Cook the chorizo in one big piece, then remove the skin and slice it. When the red pepper is tender, add the chorizo to it and grill them together for a few minutes.

When the centre of the tortilla is not too runny, slip it onto a plate, put the pan on the top of the plate, then flip the plate over in order to turn the tortilla without breaking it.

When the tortilla is ready, add the chorizo and red peppers (warm or cold) to your green leaves. Season with a good olive oil, salt and pepper.

Breakfast: Green tea, bread, butter and jam
Lunch: Veal saltimbocca, warm green bean salad
Dinner: Plate *fraîcheur*, burrata, watermelon, melon,
Parma ham, rocket salad, black olive tapenade

BREAKFAST

Bread toast   Green tea
Butter and jam

LUNCH

2 escalopes of veal of around 180g   ½ glass of Madeira wine (or Sherry
each (can be replaced by chicken)   or Port wine)
4 slices of Parma ham   400g fresh green beans
A few leaves of sage   Olive oil, salt and pepper
                                         Knob of butter

Roll each of your escalopes in two slices of Parma ham. They have to
be nearly all covered. In a frying pan, cook them with olive oil on a low
heat. Meanwhile, bring some salty water to the boil and cook the green
beans for 10 minutes, then stop the heat, cover and let them in hot
water for 5/10 minutes (according to your taste), that way they will be a
bit crunchy.

When the meat is nearly cooked till the inside (you'll have to check
by cutting in the middle with a knife), turn up the heat and pour the
wine in the pan to deglaze. Let it cook for a few more minutes with a
knob of butter; it will be golden, a bit caramelized with the sweet wine.

Season your beans with olive oil, salt and pepper when they are still
warm. Add a sage leaf on the top of each *escalope* for decoration and a
lovely taste.

DINNER

1 burrata
half of a small watermelon
half of a melon
2 slices of Parma ham
200g rocket leaves
200g black olives

2 or 3 anchovies
50g capers in brine
A few slices of old bread
Olive oil
A few leaves of basil

Prepare the black olive tapenade by blending the olives, anchovies and capers with olive oil. Blend to obtain a paste; don't add any salt, as the anchovies and capers already are salty enough). If it's too thick, add some olive oil to get a smooth paste.

Cut the old baguette or any bread in slices and toast them. Spread the olive paste on them.

After that, it's all up to you and your liking to make assemble and make this dish look delicious.

I would personally slice the watermelon, dice the melon, open the burrata in two, place the rocket leaves first, spread onto the plate, the burrata in the centre, on one side of the melon, the watermelon on the other side, in between the Parma ham in *chiffonade* and the toast of black olive tapenade.

Finish with a good drizzle of good olive oil and a few basil leaves.

Breakfast: Black coffee, oat meal with coconut flakes and fresh peach
Lunch: Summer braised chicken with tomato and polenta
Dinner: Courgette flan, quinoa, prawns and cucumber salad

BREAKFAST

Black coffee
Oatmeal cooked in milk
A pinch of coconut flakes

1 peach (either to put in your porridge or to eat just so)

LUNCH

2 shallots
2 chicken legs
150ml chicken stock
1 garlic clove
A few sprigs of thyme
200g cherry tomatoes
2 plum tomatoes quartered
200g can of cannellini beans

Half a green chilli, finely sliced
85g fine grain polenta
40g parmesan cheese grated
knob of butter
Small bunch of basil
Salt, pepper
Vegetable oil

Heat oven to 180°.

Heat 1 tbsp of the oil in a shallow ovenproof saucepan on medium heat. Throw in the shallots and soften, then remove and set aside. Season the chicken, turn up the heat and add to the pan with the remaining oil, browning all over. Return the shallots to the dish, pour over the stock and add the garlic, thyme, tomatoes, beans and chilli. Bring to the boil, cover and put in the oven for 30 mins or until the chicken is cooked through. Remove the lid and cook for 10 mins more to reduce the sauce. Meanwhile, pour the polenta into 350ml boiling water while whisking. Cook for 2 mins (or according to pack instructions). Season generously with salt, remove from the heat and stir through the Parmesan and butter. Serve the polenta with the chicken on top, scattered with basil.

DINNER

5 long courgettes
1 and a half onion

250ml liquid cream
2 eggs

60g quinoa
150g raw prawns
¼ of cucumber halved and sliced
50g green leaves
1 garlic clove

Vinaigrette with chilli: olive oil, vinegar, salt, pepper, a tsp Dijon mustard and a few chilli flake if you like it.

Wash and dice the courgettes, slice the onion finely, heat a frying pan with olive oil and on medium heat cook half of the onion and courgettes for around 15 minutes till they are soft.

Meanwhile, in another pan, cook the rest of the onion, boil 120g salty water, pour the quinoa in a salad bowl, mix with the onion and pour the water on top. Cover and let the water to be absorbed.

Preheat the oven at 180°C.

Mix the eggs with the cream, with salt and pepper, stir gently, butter generously a loaf baking tin of around 20cm by 10 and pour the courgettes mix in it. Bake for 25 minutes, then stick a knife in the middle to check if it's cooked. When out of the oven, cover the mould with a kitchen cloth: this will help your flan to come out of the mould.

Meanwhile, in another pan, heat some oil and cook the raw prawns with the garlic at once. From grey they will turn pink, when they are all pink they are ready, don't overcook your prawns.

Mix your vinaigrette and lettuce by hand (the leaves will be well covered with the sauce. Serve the prawns hot on the top with the cucumber and some slices of the flan.

Shopping List for Days Five, Six, and Seven for two people

- Yoghurt
- Blueberries
- Fresh peaches
- 2 salmon fillets of 150g each
- 200g fresh peas
- 2 big beetroot, already cooked
- 1 garlic clove
- ¼ tsp cumin
- Squeeze of a lemon
- 200g rocket salad
- 2 apricots
- 100g feta cheese
- 6 garlic cloves
- 45g fresh ginger
- A large pinch of chilli flakes (or 2 red chillies)
- About 2 tbsp tomato paste
- 1 tsp turmeric
- 2 tsp garam masala
- 1 tbsp sugar
- 750g tomatoes
- 1 teaspoon sea salt
- Freshly ground black pepper
- 200g smoked salmon
- 4 slices of brown bread
- 1 500g box of lasagna pasta
- 1 courgette
- 1 red bell pepper
- 1 aubergine
- 1 tomato
- 1 onion
- 1 ball of mozzarella
- 200g *Gruyère* cheese or similar
- 500ml milk
- 70g flour
- 100g butter
- 250g aubergine
- 1 pepper
- Half an onion
- 2 tomatoes
- 30ml cider vinegar + 30ml water
- 1 pinch of sugar
- 25g green olives pitted
- 25g capers
- 1 small bunch of celery
- 400g beef for skewers (sirloin is very good)
- Skewers sticks (if these are wood they'll have to be immersed in water the day before or at least a few hours in advance to avoid them burning when cooking)
- 2 lemons
- cumin seeds
- 400g chicken breast
- 4 fine slices of Parma ham
- 250g *Gruyère* cheese
- 200g breadcrumbs
- 150g heirloom tomatoes
- 400g rice
- 150g mozzarella
- 200g tomato sauce
- Green salad leaves of your choice
- Salt and pepper

List of basics from your pantry

- Green tea
- Black coffee
- 9 eggs
- A handful of hazelnuts
- 200g chickpeas
- Tomato coulis

- Tomato paste
- Olive oil
- *Herbes de Provence*
- 1 beef or vegetable stock cube
- Dry oregano

For Day Five, the hummus can be made way in advance, the chutney too. Actually, I would advise you to make the chutney in advance, even double the proportions as you can keep for weeks in the fridge, and of course, it's delicious anytime.

For Day Six, the vegetarian lasagna and the caponata (which is a bit like a ratatouille) and can be made days in advance, the beef skewers can be made 2 days in advance too except the *marinade,*

For Day Seven, the cordon bleus as well as the arancini can be prepared days in advance; for the arancini you can at least cook your rice. The tomato sauce can be (or should I say 'must be'?) prepared in advance.

Breakfast: Green tea, 2 poached eggs, yoghurt with fresh blueberries
Lunch: Salmon mi-cuit, pink hummus and lemon fresh peas
Dinner: Rocket salad with fresh apricots, roasted
hazelnuts, feta and tomato chutney on toast

BREAKFAST

Green tea

2 eggs

Yoghurt with a handful of
blueberries

Boil some water and plunge 2 eggs in the boiling water with a
tablespoon so as not to break the eggs. Leave them in simmering water
for 7 minutes and take off the shell carefully. Your eggs will be cooked
on the outside and runny on the inside.

LUNCH

2 salmon fillets of 150g each
200g fresh peas
2 big beetroots, already cooked
200g chickpeas
1 garlic clove

¼ tsp cumin powder
Squeeze of lemon
Olive oil
Salt and pepper
Knob of butter

Take the fresh peas out of the pods, boil some salted water. When it's
boiling, plunge the peas for 10 minutes. When they are tender, prepare
a salad bowl with ice cubes and water, and put them in cold water to
keep their beautiful green colour.

In a blender, mix the chickpeas, beetroot, garlic clove, cumin and
squeeze of lemon. Add a bit of olive oil if too thick and mix till you
obtain a smooth paste.

Heat some olive oil in a pan on high heat, cook the salmon fillets on
both sides. Make sure that the middle is still pink, unless you don't like
it that way.

When the salmon is cooked, in the same pan, reduce the heat, put a
bit of olive oil, add a knob of butter and reheat the peas in butter.

DINNER

200g rocket salad
2 apricots
100g feta cheese
A handful of hazelnuts
2 slices of brown bread
Olive oil
6 garlic cloves
45g fresh ginger

A large pinch of chilli flakes (or 2 red chillies)
2 tbsp tomato paste
1 tsp turmeric
2 tsp garam masala
1 tbsp of sugar
750g tomatoes
Teaspoon of sea salt
Freshly ground black pepper

Prepare the chutney first by smashing the garlic with the flat of a knife, peel, and chop roughly. Peel and finely grate the ginger. (Wash and finely chop the chilli if using.) Wash, core, and chop the tomatoes.

In a large heavy saucepan, heat a few tablespoons of olive oil over medium heat. Once hot, add the garlic, ginger, and chilli. Cook, stirring regularly, for a couple of minutes, until fragrant. Add the tomato paste, spices, and sugar, and cook, stirring, for another minute. Now add the tomatoes, the salt, and a good grind of pepper and mix well, scraping the pan to incorporate all the spices. Turn down the heat and simmer for about 45 minutes, until the tomatoes are thoroughly cooked and the chutney has thickened.

Meanwhile, wash the rocket salad, crush the hazelnuts in big chunks, heat a frying pan and roast them in olive oil on low heat. Meanwhile, crumble the feta on your rocket, toast your slices of bread, wash and cut the apricots in quarters, assemble all the ingredients, put your chutney on your toast and season your salad.

Breakfast: Green tea, smoked salmon and butter on brown bread
Lunch: Vegetarian lasagna with green salad
Dinner: Caponata on toast with marinated beef skewers

BREAKFAST

Green tea   Brown bread toast
150g smoked salmon

LUNCH

1 box of 500g lasagna pasta   200g cheese like *Gruyère*, grated
1 courgette   Salt and pepper
1 red bell paper   Olive oil
1 aubergine   100g butter
1 tomato   500ml milk
1 mozzarella ball   70g flour

Dice the courgette, the red bell pepper, the aubergine, slice the onion and tomato, and grate your cheese. Cut the mozzarella into cubes. Heat some olive oil in a frying pan and put the courgettes and aubergines at the same time, cook for 10 minutes on low heat and add the onion till everything is soft and the onion translucent. Preheat the oven at 180°C.

Meanwhile, prepare your bechamel sauce...

When the béchamel sauce and the vegetables are ready, butter a baking tray either with butter or oil. First spread the lasagna pasta over the base in order to cover the whole tray, then add a bit of your vegetable mix, then the béchamel sauce then some pasta again, and do the round of vegetables, béchamel sauce, pasta, etc., to the top. Ideally you should finish with some leftover béchamel sauce, the tomato slices then the grated cheese. Put in the oven for 45 minutes.

DINNER

250g aubergines

1 red bell pepper

Half an onion

2 tomatoes

30ml cider vinegar + 30ml water

2 tbsp of olive oil

A pinch of sugar

25g green olives pitted

25g capers

1 small bunch of celery

400g beef skewers

Skewers sticks

2 lemons

A pinch of cumin seeds

Salt and pepper

4 tbsp of olive oil

Skewers sticks

Dice your beef into cubes of around 2cm, unless your butcher was kind enough to do it for you. Toast the cumin seeds in a pan with no oil, for 5 minutes to enhance the flavour. In a salad bowl, mix the beef cubes with the cumin seeds, olive oil, salt and pepper and the juice of the two lemons.

Prepare your caponata if you haven't done it in advance. In a small saucepan, boil some water and plunge the tomatoes for 20 seconds. Drain them and take the skin off, cut them in half, deseed and dice them.

Cut the aubergine and pepper in little cubes, heat 1 tbsp of olive oil in a pan and cook for 15 minutes. In another pan, heat the second spoon of oil, slice the onion finely and fry the onion. When they are cooked, add the tomatoes and simmer for 10 minutes. Add the capers and olive. Slice the celery and add it the pan, stir and add the aubergine and pepper mix. Wet with the vinegar and water, season with salt and pepper, simmer for 15 more minutes till it thicken a bit and set aside. You can have the caponata warm or cold.

Skewer your beef on the sticks: heat some olive oil in a pan and fry your skewers unless you have a barbecue and can cook them on the barbecue which is ideal. The beef skewers hot with the cold caponata is just sublime.

Breakfast: Black coffee, fried eggs and baguette
Lunch: *Cordons bleus,* heirloom tomato salad
Dinner: Arancini with tomato sauce and green leaves

BREAKFAST

Black coffee

4 eggs

French bread

LUNCH

2 chicken breasts of 180g each

2 slices of cooked ham

4 or 6 pieces of cheddar cheese

100g breadcrumbs

1 egg

2 big heirloom tomatoes

Olive oil

Salt and pepper

Spread your chicken breast on a chopping board, flatten them by putting a film on them and 'beat' the breast with a pestle or a pastry roll or even the palm of your hand, to make them thinner. Take the film off, spread the ham slices on them then the cheese, fold them in half and set aside. Crack your eggs on a soup plate, whisk with a fork, add salt and pepper, on another soup plate, pour the breadcrumbs, add salt and pepper, mix with a fork.

Heat some oil in a pan, roll your chicken breasts first in the eggs, then in the breadcrumbs and put them on the frying pan, the sealed side down, first for 2/3 minutes, depending on the thickness of your chicken, and then the other side for the same time.

Meanwhile, slice your tomatoes. I let you season it the way you like it but to me, olive oil and salt are best for heirloom tomatoes.

DINNER

400g rice

150g mozzarella

100g breadcrumbs

2 eggs

200ml tomato coulis

1tbsp of tomato paste

1 onion

1 garlic clove

Olive oil

Salt and pepper

Herbes de Provence (and/or dry oregano, if you like it)

Vegetable or beef stock cube

Prepare the tomato sauce (if not prepared in advance), peel and slice the onion and garlic, fry the onion on low heat in a pan with olive oil, then add the garlic when the onion is translucent. Fry for a few minutes, add the tomato paste, and mix and pour the tomato coulis, season with salt, pepper and *herbes de Provence* and/or dry oregano. Let it simmer on low heat; if it gets too thick, add some water. While it simmers, boil 500ml of salted water in a saucepan and cook the rice (if not made ready in advance). Drain the rice well and let it to cool down.

Dice the mozzarella into small cubes.

When rice is cold, you have two ways to make your arancini:

1: You mix the rice with the tomato sauce and the mozzarella cubes.

2: You add only the mozzarella to the rice. When the arancini are ready, you spread the tomato sauce on the top...

As I love tomato sauce, I would put some everywhere. The more there is, the best it is for me, so I usually make a lot of tomato sauce, mix my rice with it, and when the arancini are done, I also spread the rest of the tomato sauce on top.

The proportions I gave you should be all right to have enough tomato sauce both inside and outside the arancini.

Let's say you chose the second option: you mix your rice with tomato sauce, add the mozzarella cubes and mix gently till your rice is red but not too wet. Take two bowls or soup plates: in one, you crack your eggs and mix with salt and pepper; in the second one, put the breadcrumbs with salt and pepper and mix with a fork.

With your hands, form some balls with your rice of around 10cm diameter. When they are all done, set aside in the fridge for at least half an hour.

Then roll each ball in eggs first and breadcrumbs and do the same round again (eggs and breadcrumbs). Doing it two times will form a more solid and crunchy crust.

Heat some vegetable oil in a saucepan (2cm high) to nearly deep-fry your arancini.

Fry them and drain on paper napkins. Season and heat with your green salad and the dressing of your choice.

AUTUMN

Day	Breakfast	Lunch	Dinner	Well-being
1	Black coffee, croissant or *pain au chocolat*	Sweet potato, grilled chickpeas with lemon, tahini sauce	Chicory salad with ham, walnuts, and *Roquefort* or *Gruyère* cheese	☐ water ☐ sport/walk ☐ mindfulness ☐ pleasure
2	Green tea, bread, butter and jam tartines	Croque monsieur with Parma ham, baby spinach salad	Butternut squash soup, cream cheese tartine	☐ water ☐ sport/walk ☐ mindfulness ☐ pleasure
3	Oatmeal with fresh apples and hazelnuts	Mushroom and fresh herb omelette with whole roasted cauliflower	Hot goat cheese salad, leek and beetroot	☐ water ☐ sport/walk ☐ mindfulness ☐ pleasure
4	Black coffee, fried eggs and bread	Sirloin steak *à l'échalotte* and roasted baby potatoes with garlic	Autumn lentil salad, roasted pumpkin, pomegranate and watercress	☐ water ☐ sport/walk ☐ mindfulness ☐ pleasure
5	Green tea, croissant or *pain au chocolat*	Brown bread *tartines* with mushrooms and poached eggs on green salad	Parsnips and broccoli soup	☐ water ☐ sport/walk ☐ mindfulness ☐ pleasure
6	Black coffee, natural yoghurt, fresh berries	Rosemary lamb cutlets and butternut squash tian	One pot mixed vegetable soup	☐ water ☐ sport/walk ☐ mindfulness ☐ pleasure
7	Black coffee, poached eggs, yoghurt	Spanish-style cod	One thousand virtues salad	☐ water ☐ sport/walk ☐ mindfulness ☐ pleasure

Shopping List for Days One, Two, Three and Four for two people

- 1 big sweet potato or 2 small
- 1 lemon (zests and juice)
- 2 tbsp of Greek yoghurt
- 2 tbsp of tahini paste
- A few rocket leaves
- A few sprigs of coriander chopped
- 2 big chicories
- 2 slices of cooked ham
- 100g *Roquefort* or *Gruyère* cheese
- 10 large slices of brown bread or grains bread
- 2 slices of Parma ham
- 2 slices of Reblochon cheese (or *Morbier* or *Tomme* cheese)
- 100g grated cheese like *Gruyère* or Cheddar
- 1 butternut squash
- 150g cream cheese
- A few sprigs of chives
- 250g mushrooms
- A few sprigs of parsley
- 1 cooked beetroot
- 2 small leeks
- 1 orange
- 1 whole cauliflower
- 150g creamy goat cheese
- 1 cooked beetroot
- 1 orange (zests and juice)
- 1 leek
- 2 sirloin steaks of 170g each
- 12 shallots
- 4 handful of baby potatoes
- 400g lentils
- 1 pumpkin
- Half of a pomegranate
- 4 handful of watercress

List of basics from your pantry

- Black coffee
- Green tea
- Oatmeal
- 2 onions
- 250g chickpeas
- 2 garlic cloves
- 8 eggs
- A handful of walnuts
- Olive oil
- 3 knobs of butter
- 1 tsp Dijon mustard
- 50g butter
- 50g flour
- 60cl of milk
- 1 tbsp of honey
- 1 tsp paprika
- 1 vegetable stock cube

For your week ahead, dishes you may prepare in advance:

For Days One and Two, you can prepare you chickpeas, and tahini sauce, cut all the ingredients for the dinner salad that you will assemble at the last minute, like in restaurants. The croque monsieur can be made in advance and cooked at the last minute, like the butternut squash soup.

For Day Three, The mushrooms for the omelette can be cooked in advance too. Think that for Day Three the cauliflower needs to cook at least for an hour. Baking it in advance is possible but to me, it's even nicer when it's hot from the oven.

For Day Four, the shallots can be prepared days in advance, as well as the lentils for the evening, you'll just have to add the other vegetables at the last minute.

Day One

Breakfast: Black coffee, croissant or *pain au chocolat*
Lunch: Roasted sweet potato, grilled chickpeas with lemon, tahini sauce
Dinner: Chicory salad with ham, walnuts,
and *Roquefort* or *Gruyère* cheese

BREAKFAST
Black coffee   2 croissants or *pains au chocolat*

LUNCH

1 big sweet potato (or 2 small)   2 tbsp of Greek yoghurt
250g chickpeas   2 tbsp of tahini paste
1 Half an onion   A few rocket leaves
1 lemon (zests and juice)   A few sprigs of coriander, chopped
                                         Half of a pomegranate

Preheat your oven at 180°C.

    Wash and brush your potato under water (no need to peel them, especially if they are organic), roll it in baking paper or foil.

    Put in the oven for around 1 hour (depending on the size).

Meanwhile, drain your chickpeas. Zest your lemon and juice it.

Slice your onion, heat some olive oil in a pan and cook your onion till it's translucent. Then add the chickpeas to it, let them grill a little, they have to become brown, mash half of them roughly with a fork. Deseed the pomegranate, and prepare your tahini sauce by mixing the tahini and yoghurt with a bit of lemon juice and salt and pepper. The sauce has to be thick. Wash the rocket leaves, and wash and chop the coriander.

When the sweet potato is ready, cut it in half, put the chickpeas on the top with the rest of lemon juice, the lemon zests, coriander, rocket leaves and pomegranate. At the last minute pour some tahini sauce on the top and drizzle the whole potato with olive oil.

DINNER

2 big chicories	100g *Roquefort* or *Gruyère* cheese
2 slices of cooked ham	1 handful of walnuts

Wash and slice the chicories. Cut your ham in big pieces as well as the cheese.

In a salad bowl, mix all the ingredients with the walnuts and season to your taste (the best to me is a dressing with lemon and olive oil).

Breakfast: Green tea, bread, butter and jam tartines
Lunch: *Croque Monsieur* with Parma ham, baby spinach salad
Dinner: Butternut squash soup, cream cheese tartine

BREAKFAST

Green tea
Bread

Butter
Jam

LUNCH

4 large slices of brown bread or grains bread
2 slices of Parma ham
2 slices of *Reblochon* cheese (or *Morbier* or *Tomme* cheese)
100g grated cheese like *Gruyère* or cheddar

50g butter
50g flour
60cl of milk
A knob of butter
1 tsp Dijon mustard

Preheat your oven at 180°C.

Spread the Dijon mustard on two slices of bread and the butter on the others.

Cut your cheese in thin rectangles.

Make your *bechamel* sauce: Melt your butter in a saucepan, then sprinkle the flour and whisk, when the *roux* is made (it has to be a very soft 'dough', nearly liquid) add the milk slowly by whisking. Set aside when it's still had a custard consistency, it will harden a bit when cold.

For one *Croque Monsieur*, you'll need two slices (one with the mustard, the other with the butter). Take the slice with the mustard and spread the cheese in rectangles in order to cover the whole slice and do the same with the Parma ham. Cover with around two tbsp of *béchamel* sauce, close the Croque Monsieur with the buttered slice and spread some grated cheese on the top.

Put both *Croques Monsieur* in the oven for around 15 minutes, till both cheeses (the one inside and the one on the top) have melted. Wash and season your baby spinach and enjoy the *Croque Monsieur* the French way, with green salad.

DINNER

1 butternut squash	150g cream cheese
1 onion	2 sprigs of chives
1 vegetable stock cube	Olive oil
2 slices of white or brown bread	

Peel and slice the onion. Peel and cut the butternut squash in small chunks.

Heat some olive oil in a pan, and cook both ingredients together on low heat.

Prepare your bouillon by boiling 500ml of water and the stock cube.

If the butternut and onion start to become brown but still hard, pour a bit of the bouillon, that way they won't burn.

When the butternut is soft put them in a blender, add some bouillon on the top and blitz till obtaining a silk soup. Check the seasoning, add some more bouillon if you want your soup to be more liquid.

You can either toast your bread or not (toasted is best to me!) and spread the cream cheese on it and eat your tartines with your soup.

Breakfast: Black coffee, oatmeal with fresh apple slices and hazelnuts

Lunch: Mushroom and fresh herb omelette
with whole roasted cauliflower

Dinner: Hot goat cheese salad, leek and beetroot

BREAKFAST

Black coffee	Butter
Oat meal	Jam

LUNCH

250g mushrooms	Olive oil
4 eggs	Salt and pepper
A few sprigs of parsley	1 garlic clove
1 cauliflower	Salt and pepper

Preheat your oven at 180°C. Rince the cauliflower, take off the leaves and keep them (especially if it's organic). Spread some baking paper or foil (baking paper is always healthier). Put your cauliflower in the middle with the leaves, sprinkle the paprika, add salt pepper and olive oil, close the paper in order to cover and seal the cauliflower completely. Put in the oven for at least 1h (depends on the size) but the cauliflower has to be very soft at heart.

Wash and chop your mushrooms, add the garlic clove diced, heat a frying pan and cook the mushrooms and garlic for around min.

Wash and chop the parsley.

Meanwhile, crack the eggs in a bowl, add salt and pepper and whisk with a fork.

When the mushrooms are cooked, put them in the bowl with eggs and add the parsley. In the same frying pan, add a bit more olive oil and pour your mushrooms and eggs mix. When one side is cooked you can fold the omelette and leave it runny if like it that way, if not fold it and cook both sides till the eggs inside are completely cooked.

DINNER

2 slices of brown bread
150g creamy goat cheese
2 handful of watercress
1 cooked beetroot

2 small leeks
A knob of butter
Olive oil
1 orange

Slice your leeks finely, let them soak in fresh water and rinse them. Leeks are difficult to wash because of the soil inside, but if you slice them first you won't have any soil anymore.

In a frying pan, heat some olive oil and butter and cook your leeks on low heat.

Meanwhile preheat your oven at 180°C. Slice your goat cheese and put it on your bread slices.

Put your *tartines* in the oven for 10 minutes till the cheese has melted.

Zest your orange, wash the watercress, press your orange to add the juice in your dressing. Dice your beetroot and let it marinate in the orange juice dressing (olive oil, salt, pepper and orange juice).

Eat your goat cheese *tartines* hot, with your cold or warm leek and cold beetroot on the top of the watercress.

Breakfast: Black coffee, fried eggs and bread
Lunch: Sirloin steak *à l'échalote* and roasted baby potatoes with garlic
Dinner: Autumn lentil salad, roasted pumpkin,
pomegranate and watercress

BREAKFAST

Black coffee   Baguette
4 eggs

LUNCH

2 sirloin steaks of around 170g   1 big knob of butter
each   1 garlic clove
12 shallots   Olive oil
4 handfuls of baby potatoes

Boil half a litre of salted water, when boiling plunge the potatoes that you had rinsed in advance. When soft (after around 10 minutes), turn off the heat and keep aside.

Meanwhile, peel and slice your shallots finely. Heat a frying pan with olive oil and cook the shallots on low heat. If it starts to burn and the shallots are still not cooked (they have to be soft and translucent), add a bit of water. When cooked, add a knob of butter and cook your sirloin on the same pan to give the meat the taste of shallots.

Peel and slice the garlic very finely. Take another pan and fry the potatoes on high heat with some olive oil (just to brown them as they are already cooked) with the garlic. When the potatoes are brown, add a knob of butter for the taste, salt and pepper and add them to the pan with meat and shallots.

DINNER

400g lentils
1 small pumpkin
Half a pomegranate
Half an onion
2 handfuls of watercress

2 sprigs of parsley
Olive oil
1 vegetable bouillon cube
Salt and pepper

Heat your oven at 180°C. Cut the pumpkin in slices and peel. Take the seeds out (you can keep them to roast and add to your salad), spread the slices on a baking tray with baking paper, add olive oil, salt and pepper and cook for around 20 minutes (till the pumpkin is soft).

Dice the onion very finely, wash and chop the parsley.

In a pan, boil 500ml of water add the bouillon cube to it and let it dissolve.

In a frying pan, cook the onion with olive oil. When the onion is translucent, pour the lentils, mix well with the onion and cover with some bouillon.

Let it simmer: the water will be absorbed by the lentils. Check them, and if they are still hard, add a bit of water. Add more water, little by little, till the lentils are soft. Stop the heat and cover. Deseed the pomegranate.

When the pumpkin slices are cooked, cut them into cubes, add them to the lentils, along with the pomegranate. Put the watercress on the side of a plate with a bit of olive oil, and serve the warm lentils next to it.

Shopping List for Days Five, Six and Seven for two people

- 2 large slices of white or brown bread
- 250g mushrooms
- Rocket or any green leaves
- A few sprigs of parsley
- 1 small broccoli
- 4 parsnips
- 2 spoonsful of crème fraîche (optional but nice)
- Fresh berries
- 6 lamb cutlets
- 2 sprigs of fresh rosemary
- 1 butternut
- 1 big carrot chopped
- 6 celery stalks
- 2 tbsp of sweet corn from a tin
- 85g red or white beans

List of basics from your pantry

- Black coffee
- Green tea
- 4 eggs
- 4 vegetables stock cube
- 3 onions
- 35g butter + 1 knob
- 20g flour
- 2 garlic cloves
- 120ml milk
- ½ tsp salt
- 1 pinch of oregano
- 1 pinch of fresh thyme (if not, use dry one)

For your week ahead, dishes you may prepare in advance:

For Day Five, you can prepare your mushrooms, even the poached eggs, they can be preserved in a box with cold water in the fridge, the soup for dinner can be ready even days in advance and again, make some more (see the batch cooking chapter on page 131)

For Day Six, the butternut squash tian can be prepared in advance, either precooked or raw in a baking tray, ready to go in the oven. The one pot vegetable soup as well.

For Day Seven, the cod can be all prepared the day before in a baking tray covered with film and ready to be baked as it will cook all at once.

Breakfast: Green tea, croissant or *pain au chocolat*
Lunch: Brown bread *tartines* with mushrooms
and poached eggs on green salad
Dinner: Parsnips and broccoli soup

BREAKFAST

Green tea   Croissant or *pain au chocolat*

LUNCH

2 large slices of white or brown
bread
250g mushrooms
Rocket or any green leaves
1 garlic clove

2 eggs
Olive oil
A few sprigs of parsley
Salt and pepper

Wash and chop the mushrooms, heat a frying pan and cook them with
a bit of olive oil, salt and pepper. Peel and dice the garlic very finely, add
it to the mushrooms.

Meanwhile, boil some water with salt. When boiling reduce the heat
on low and crack one egg and turn the water slowly with a spoon, the
egg will form a nice ball and the white won't go everywhere in the

water. The easier is to poach the eggs one by one, leave the first one for 6 min, scoop it with a small sieve or spoon and let it rest on a paper towel while you cook the other one also for 6 min, if the first egg is cold just plunge it again for 10 seconds in the hot water.

Wash the green leaves, spread the salad on a plate, the bread slices on the top, when the mushrooms are cooked (which will be approximately the time for cooking the eggs), pour them on the bread, then the eggs on the top, add a drizzle of olive oil and it's ready.

DINNER

1 small broccoli
4 parsnips
1 onion
1 vegetable stock cube

2 spoonful of *crème fraîche* (optional but delicious)
Olive oil
Salt and pepper

Boil 500ml of salted water and dissolve the stock cube when the water is hot. Meanwhile, peel the parsnips and wash and cut the broccoli into small florets. Either put the broccoli and parsnips on a baking tray or in a pan with olive oil. Soups are always better if you roast or fry your vegetables in a pan, it gives more taste.

If you are using the oven, preheat it at 180°C, drizzle with olive oil, salt and pepper and bake for around 20 minutes till the vegetables are soft.

When soft, put them in the blender and blend with the bouillon till you obtain the right consistency.

At the last minute, spoon the cold *crème fraîche* on the top: it's bliss!

Breakfast: Black coffee, natural yoghurt, fresh berries
Lunch: Rosemary lamb cutlets and butternut squash tian
Dinner: One pot mixed vegetable soup

BREAKFAST

Black coffee   Mixed red berries
Natural yoghurt

LUNCH

6 lamb cutlets   Half an onion
2 sprigs of fresh rosemary   1 vegetable stock cube
1 butternut squash

Boil 500ml of salted water and dissolve the stock cube in it. Preheat the oven at 180°C.

Wash your butternut and keep the skin on (especially if it is organic). Cut in half and take out the seeds. (Again, if you can put them aside them to roast and put on a salad, it's great: wash them in running water, put in a bowl with salt, pepper, olive oil, paprika and/or the spice you like and roast in a pan for a few minutes, till it smells delicious and the seeds are getting golden brown.)

For the butternut itself, slice it very very finely (ideally with a mandoline – it's quicker and easier). Peel and slice the onion very finely. Place the butternut slices on a baking tray with slices of onions in between but place the butternut not flat, not straight but in between: start from one side of the tray, tilt the butternut and slide some onion slices inside.

Drizzle some olive oil, salt and pepper and pour some bouillon in order to cover the butter a third of the way. Bake for around 30 minutes, till the butternut is very soft. Meanwhile, heat a frying pan on high heat with a bit of olive oil, put some salt and pepper on each of your cutlets (both sides) and grill with the rosemary on the side in your pan till the cutlets brown and get a bit pink in the middle.

It's important to leave the rosemary in sprigs, otherwise you'll have thorns of rosemary everywhere. When the meat is cooked, stop and cover with a lid or baking paper to enhance the flavour of the rosemary in the meat. Eat hot with the butternut *tian* that should melt in the mouth.

DINNER

1 big carrot
6 celery stalks
2 tbsp of sweet corn (from a tin)
Half an onion
1 vegetable stock cube
85g red or white beans (from a tin)
20g flour
2 garlic cloves

120ml milk
½ tsp salt
1 pinch of oregano
1 pinch of fresh thyme (if not, use dry one)
35g butter
Olive oil

Boil 500ml of salted water and dissolve the stock cube in it. Heat some olive oil in a pot on medium heat. Slice the onion and cook with the carrots and celery stalks chopped, the garlic cloves crushed and salt and pepper. Cook for 5 minutes or until the onions are translucent. Add the butter: once it starts to melt, combine the flour and mix covering the vegetables in flour. This roux mixture will be thick and sticky.

Slowly add the vegetable stock, oregano, thyme, and rosemary and mix until well combined.

Stir the soup frequently until the soup comes to a gentle boil. As the soup heats up you will start to see it thicken. Make sure to keep stirring so the soup does not burn and doesn't make any lumps. Then add the corn, the beans and milk. Cook on low heat for 10 minutes.

Breakfast: Black coffee, poached eggs, yoghurt
Lunch: Spanish-style cod
Dinner: One thousand virtues salad

BREAKFAST

Black coffee
2 eggs

Natural yoghurt

LUNCH

2 cod fillet of 150g each
600ml tomato coulis
400g white beans
180g black olives pitted

Half of a white onion
1 red bell pepper
½ strong chorizo
Salt and pepper

Preheat the oven at 180°C. Slice the onion, red bell pepper and black olives. Put the white beans and tomato coulis on a baking tray, add salt and pepper. Take the skin off the chorizo, then slice it. Add it to the tray with pepper, onion and olive and mix. Put salt and pepper on both sides of the fish, place the fish on the top and put in the oven at 180°C for 30/45 minutes.

DINNER

4 big leaves of kale
5 Brussels sprouts
2 tbsp of quinoa
A few almonds
Around 6 shiitake mushrooms
Half of a garlic clove
30g parmesan cheese
1 tbsp of pumpkin seeds or linseeds
50g tofu
1 handful of watercress
1 orange
1 tbsp of olive oil
1 handful of fresh parsley

1 tbsp of colza oil
1 tbsp of olive oil
2 tbsp of soy sauce
1 tbsp of cider vinegar
1 pinch of hot chilli flakes (optional)
Black pepper

Boil some water with salt, wash your kale leaves and take off the white part if too thick. (Keep it for a soup.) Cook the leaves for 4 minutes, drain and set aside. Keep the water and plunge the quinoa in it (gain of time, no water wasted). Wash and chop the Brussel sprouts after taking off the first few leaves (with a mandoline or very sharp knife).

Meanwhile, crush the almonds, shave the parmesan, zest the orange and juice it. Put the tofu in the soy sauce to marinate. Wash the watercress. Chop the shiitake and dice the garlic finely. In a pan, heat some olive oil and cook the mushrooms and garlic for 5 minutes on high heat with a few drops of soy sauce. Add some black pepper, the chilli flakes (if you want them) and the parsley, roughly chopped. Reduce the heat and cook for five more minutes.

Meanwhile, mix the soy sauce, the orange juice in a bowl, adding the cider vinegar and colza oil. On your plate, put the kale leaves, then the watercress, quinoa, the Brussels sprouts, then the tofu into cubes and the parmesan shaves. Sprinkle with the almonds, orange zests and pumpkin seeds.

WINTER

Day	Breakfast	Lunch	Dinner	Well-being
1	Green tea, brown bread toasted, butter and jam	Parmesan cheese and lemon zest crust baked cod with brown rice	Spinach and halloumi casserole with artisan baguette and lemon	☐ water ☐ sport/walk ☐ mindfulness ☐ pleasure
2	Black coffee, fresh baguette, butter and jam	Citrus and honey chicken baked with rosemary, baked French fries	Onion soup with croutons and grated cheese	☐ water ☐ sport/walk ☐ mindfulness ☐ pleasure
3	Oatmeal, coconut flakes, dried fruits, nuts, agave syrup or honey	Beef bourguignon with boiled potatoes	Butternut squash soup, Parma ham chips	☐ water ☐ sport/walk ☐ mindfulness ☐ pleasure
4	Green tea, brown bread toasted, butter and jam	Meatballs with my dad's tomato sauce and fresh pasta	My mum's potato and leek soup	☐ water ☐ sport/walk ☐ mindfulness ☐ pleasure
5	Green tea, fried eggs, baguette and bananas	Salmon steak with *béchamel* sauce and brown rice with fresh herbs	*Polenta à la Niçoise*	☐ water ☐ sport/walk ☐ mindfulness ☐ pleasure
6	Black coffee, oat flakes, banana and honey	*Gnocchi gorgonzola* and walnuts	Eggs *meurette gratin*	☐ water ☐ sport/walk ☐ mindfulness ☐ pleasure
7	Black coffee, croissant or *pain au chocolat*	*Hachis parmentier* (gratin of meat and mash potatoes), green salad	*Endives au jambon* (chicory wrapped in ham)	☐ water ☐ sport/walk ☐ mindfulness ☐ pleasure

For your week ahead, dishes you may prepare in advance:

For Day One, you can prepare the crust for the cod. The spinach casserole can be made fully in advance as it's even nicer reheated.

For Day Two, you can prepare the chicken in a roasting dish. Add the rosemary, cover and put in the fridge. You will just have to add the citrus and honey just before roasting. The onion soup can be made fully in advance as it's wonderful reheated.

For Day Three, the beef *bourguignon* can be prepared fully in advance, as ideally it needs to cook twice.

For Day Four, the meatballs can be prepared in advance and the tomato sauce will be even nicer reheated after spending a few days in the fridge. Potato and leek soup can be made in advance.

Shopping List for Days One, Two, Three and Four for two people

- 250g parmesan cheese
- 2 lemons
- 1 bouquet fresh parsley
- 1 tsp garlic powder
- 1 pound of fresh cod
- 1 bag of baby spinach
- 250g halloumi (or feta) in cubes
- 1 tsp *harissa* or finely chopped hot chilies
- 2 chicken thigh or breasts
- 1 orange
- 2 rosemary sprigs
- A few croutons
- 100g grated cheddar or Gruyère
- 2 tbsp of oats
- 1 tbsp of coconut flakes
- Dried fruits
- 400g chuck steak cut in big cubes (your butcher can cut the meat for you)
- 1 bouquet garni
- Potatoes
- 1 butternut squash
- 2 slices of Parma ham
- 500g minced beef
- Or 300g minced beef +200g minced pork
- Parsley leaves and/or cilantro
- 250g fresh pasta (penne/ spaghetti)
- 2 leeks

Basics from Your Pantry

- 1 onion
- 1 tsp paprika
- Butter
- 1 small tin of tomatoes + 1 big tin
- 1 small tin of chick peas
- Vegetable oil
- 2 vegetable bouillon/stock cubes
- 4 garlic cloves
- 1 beef or vegetable bouillon cube
- 1 tsp tomato *coulis*
- 1 splash of red or white wine
- *Herbes de Provence*

Breakfast: Green tea, brown bread toasted, butter and jam

Lunch: Parmesan cheese and lemon zest
crust baked cod with brown rice

Dinner: Spinach and halloumi casserole
with artisan baguette and lemon

BREAKFAST

Green tea   Butter
Brown bread   Homemade or good-quality jam

LUNCH

200g freshly grated parmesan cheese

1 lemon, zest + juice (organic is highly recommended as we are using the skin)

2 tbsp of chopped fresh parsley

1 tea spoon of garlic powder

1 tea spoon of paprika

3 tbsp butter, melted (can be replaced by olive oil for a lighter version)

Pinch of salt and black pepper

1 pounds of fresh cod

300g brown rice

Preheat the oven to 180°C. In a bowl, mix parmesan, lemon zest, parsley, paprika, garlic powder and salt and pepper. Put the oil (or melted butter) in another bowl.

Roll the cod in oil or butter first. Then roll it in the spices and parmesan mix. Put them on a baking tray with baking paper and cook for around 15 minutes. Meanwhile, boil some water with salt and cook the brown rice. The cod has to be flaky and translucent for a perfect taste, so it depends on the size of your fish. The cooking will be between 10 and 15 minutes.

DINNER

1 onion, sliced
1 small tin of tomatoes in juice
1 small tin of chickpeas
1 bag of baby spinach
250g halloumi cheese (or feta cheese) in cubes
1 tsp *harissa* or finely chopped hot chillies
1 lemon
Grated parmesan cheese
Olive oil
Salt and pepper to your taste
Artisan baguette

Heat a pot and pour in a splash of olive oil. Cook the onion on medium heat and, when translucent, add the tomatoes, *harissa*, salt and pepper. Mix well and add the chickpeas. Then let it simmer for five minutes. Add the halloumi or feta cubes and at the last minute, just before stopping the heat, add the baby spinach. Serve on a plate with a lemon slice on the side, parmesan cheese on the top and a drizzle of olive oil. Enjoy it with toasted baguette.

MY FRENCH SECRETS

Breakfast: Black coffee, fresh baguette, butter and jam

Lunch: Citrus and honey chicken baked
with rosemary, baked French fries

Dinner: Onion soup with croutons and grated cheese

BREAKFAST

Black coffee

Baguette

Butter

Homemade or good-quality jam

LUNCH

2 chicken thighs or breasts

1 lemon + 1 orange

2 rosemary sprigs

2 tbsp of runny honey

Salt and pepper

Olive oil

2 potatoes (like Yukon) with the skin cut into large fries

3 garlic cloves, crushed

½ tsp smoked paprika

60ml vegetable oil

2 tsp fine wheat semolina

Salt and pepper

Preheat the oven to 180°C. Season your chicken on both sides with salt and pepper. Place it on a baking tray with baking paper. Slice your orange and lemon. Put them nicely in between and around your chicken. Drizzle honey on the chicken and on the citrus to caramelise them. Squeeze the rosemary in between the chicken pieces. Drizzle with olive oil and bake for at least 45 minutes, until the chicken is cooked inside.

Meanwhile, wash and cut the potatoes. Boil some water with salt and boil the fries for five minutes in boiling water to precook them. Drain them and mix them in a bowl with the garlic, oil, semolina, paprika, salt and pepper. Spread them on a baking tray with baking paper. Put the oven on high heat at 240°C. Put the chicken at the bottom of your oven and the fries on the top. Cook the fries and chicken together for the last 35 minutes, turning the fries halfway through cooking so that they get brown on each side.

DINNER

4 brown onions
2 tbsp of flour
500ml chicken or vegetable
bouillon cube
A few croutons

100g grated cheddar or *Gruyère* cheese
Splash of red wine (optional)
Olive or vegetable oil

Slice the onions, heat a pot and add a drizzle of oil. Cook the onions on medium heat. Meanwhile, prepare the bouillon by boiling some water and adding one vegetable or chicken bouillon cube. When the onions are translucent, spread your flour on them, mix and pour the bouillon on them. Let it simmer for around 20 minutes. If you would like to add some wine to it, add it on the last five minutes of cooking. Meanwhile, prepare your croutons. (This could be from an old baguette cut into cubes, or they can be bought in French bakery sometimes. If using an old baguette, cut your bread first. Then in a bowl, mix them with a bit of olive oil, salt and pepper. Spread them on a baking tray and toast them for three minutes, turning them regularly.) Leave your oven on (still on grill option). When the soup and croutons are ready, pour the soup in a soup bowl, spread some croutons on the top, then grated cheese and place your bowls in the oven to melt and grill the cheese for half a minute.

The flour will help to thicken the soup during cooking. Without the flour, you would have a tasty but light and clear bouillon.

Breakfast: Oatmeal, coconut flakes, dried
fruits, nuts, agave syrup or honey
Lunch: Beef bourguignon with boiled potatoes
Dinner: Butternut squash soup, Parma ham chips

BREAKFAST

2 tbsp of oats
1 tbsp of coconut flakes

Dried fruits and nuts of your choice
Agave syrup or honey to your taste

Heat up the milk. When warm, turn off the heat and add the oats. Let it be on the side while you slice the banana. Add the honey and eat warm.

LUNCH

400g chuck steak cut into big cubes (Your butcher can cut the meat for you.)
1 onion
2 tbsp of flour

Half a bottle of good red wine (*pinot noir,* for example)
1 bouquet of *garni*
Vegetable oil
Salt and pepper
250g boiled potatoes

There's no need to be a good cook to make a great *boeuf bourguignon.* The secret is to marinate the meat in red wine. Then cook it slowly for hours (yes, for hours). It's something that you can prepare on your half a day prep, and if I were you, I would double the size and prepare some more, because beef *bourguignon* (like all the dishes in sauce) is so easy to freeze and defrost when late at home. And it goes well with some boiled potatoes, rice or even a mix of vegetables.

In a bowl, put your meat cubes, wine and *bouquet garni* with a bit of salt and pepper. Mix, cover and leave it in the fridge overnight.
    When you are ready to cook it, drain the meat but keep the wine. Peel and slice your onion and heat it in a frying pan with a drizzle of oil. When the onions are translucent, add the meat with salt and pepper. The meat has to be seared but not cooked inside. Make sure that each side of the meat is golden-brown. Then spread the flour on the beef and onion. Mix for one minute and pour the wine used to marinate

the meat on it. Turn the heat down, cover and let it simmer for at least three hours. If your dish is oven-proof, cover with a lid or foil and put it in a preheated oven at 180°C for at least three hours.

Check regularly to make sure there's enough liquid, and if not, add a quarter of the bottle of wine. If it bubbles too much, turn the heat down. It has to simmer, not boil. Check your seasoning after an hour or so and adjust. The sauce and meat will get brown slowly. The seasoning can be added again during the cooking anyway, so no need to add too much salt at the beginning.

Just before eating, boiled 500ml of water with salt. Peel the potatoes, cut them in four (if they are big) and boil them till tender (for around 10 minutes). Serve the meat, the potatoes and some wine sauce on the top.

DINNER

1 butternut squash
1 vegetable cube bouillon
1 onion
2 fine slices of Parma ham

Vegetable oil
Salt and pepper
Baking paper

Cut the butternut squash in half lengthwise, take out the seeds and peel it. Peel and slice the onion finely and dice the butternut into 1 cm cubes. Heat a bit of oil in a pan and put the butternut in for around 15 minutes, covered on low heat with salt and pepper.

Boil 500ml of water and add the stock cube. Mix to dissolve it.

Check the butternut. If it starts to be too dry and stick on the pan, add a little bit of bouillon. Adjust the seasoning, and add the onion slices. Cut the slices of Parma ham in straps of around 10cm long.

Preheat the oven at 180°. On a baking paper, place the Parma ham and cook for around 10 minutes, till it starts to get brown and crispy. When the butternut is soft and the onion translucent, put everything in a food processor with half of the bouillon. Blend and check the consistency; if it's too thick, add some more bouillon. It's always better to add the bouillon little by little and adjust than pour it all at once and get a soup that is too liquid. When the Parma ham is crispy, pour the soup in a nice soup bowl or plate with the Parma ham chips on the top.

Breakfast: Green tea, brown bread toasted, butter and jam
Lunch: Meatballs with my dad's tomato sauce and fresh pasta
Dinner: My mum's potato and leek soup

BREAKFAST

Green tea

Brown bread

Butter

Homemade or good-quality jam

LUNCH

For the tomato sauce:

1 brown onion
2 garlic cloves
1 beef or vegetable bouillon cube
1 tsp tomato coulis
1 big can of tomato in juice
1 splash of red or white wine
(optional)
Olive oil
Salt and pepper
Herbes de Provence

For the meatballs:

250g minced beef (your butcher
can do this) or 200g minced beef +
50g minced pork
2 garlic cloves
1 brown onion
Parsley and/or coriander
Flour
Salt and pepper
Olive or vegetable oil
250g fresh pasta like penne or
spaghetti

This recipe is for 10 meatballs, so 5 per person of around 25g each. You can either use beef only or a mix of beef and pork, which will make your balls even moister.

NUTRITIONIST'S NOTE

Coriander

The Egyptians introduced this herb to Europe and during the 18th century it was cultivated in Paris. It is the champion of digestion!

In addition to its unparalleled aromatic fragrance, coriander calms intestinal spasms, evacuates nasty little gases and helps any air accumulated in our abdomen disappear. When fresh, it is wonderful, but as a dried herb or an essential oil, it is also extremely appealing.

Prepare the sauce:

Peel and slice the onion. Peel and chop the garlic very finely. Brown them both in a pan with olive oil, and when the onion is translucent, add the tomato coulis, mix well and add the tomatoes in juice. Put the heat very low and let it simmer after adding salt and pepper. It needs to simmer for a few hours. The more it simmers, the better it will be.

When the liquid of the tomatoes disappears, add a bit of water with the bouillon cube. Taste and adjust the seasoning with *herbes de Provence* and salt and pepper. It will bubble a bit and the idea is to add a bit of water at a time. When it gets brown and dry, add some more little by little. Stay around, mix and taste regularly. Add the splash of wine at the end and stop it after a few minutes to let the alcohol evaporate. It can be prepared even a few days in advance and reheated at the last minute.

Meanwhile, prepare the meatballs by mixing the beef and pork with salt and pepper, parsley and/or coriander finely chopped. Form some balls with your hands. When you're all done, pour some flour onto a plate and roll them one by one in the flour. Heat some oil on medium heat and brown the balls on each side. When brown but still raw inside, put them in the tomato sauce to finish the cooking. At the same time, boil some water with salt to cook the pasta.

NUTRITIONIST'S NOTE

Herbes de Provence

This famous blend of Provençal herbs comes from a book by Marcel Pagnol and is known as the 'Swiss Army knife' of our culinary tradition due to its versatility. It smells of sunshine, blue skies and Mediterranean plants.

Traditionally, the blend is composed of thyme, rosemary, savoury, marjoram, basil and sometimes oregano, fennel, laurel and sage. The herbs blended together provide a mix that is typically also used as a disinfectant, a tonic, or to aid with respiration and digestion.

It offers a good way to simplify your cooking, whilst also giving it an inimitable Mediterranean flavour.

DINNER

2 potatoes, cut into big cubes   1 bouillon cube (optional)
2 leeks   Piece of butter (optional)

To wash your leeks easily, slice them before soaking them in water. That will allow a very thorough cleaning, with no trace of soil.

Boil 500ml of water and add the bouillon cube. Peel the potatoes and wash them and the leeks. When the water is boiling, put the potatoes in for around 10 minutes. When they are tender, put the leeks for five minutes more. When ready, put everything in a food processor and blend to obtain a silky soup. If the soup is too thick for you, add a bit of water.

We don't put the leeks in water at the very beginning with the potatoes as they are tender, and we do not want to boil them so that we can keep all the vitamins.

For the preparation ahead:

For Day Five, same as for Day Four, the tomato sauce can be (or has to be) prepared in advance for the *polenta.*

For Day Seven, the mash potato and meat can be prepared in advance and assembled and cooked on the day.

Shopping List for Days Five, Six and Seven for two people

- 2 salmon steaks
- 250g polenta
- 1 litre of water
- 50g parmesan cheese
- 200g mushrooms
- 1 handful of pitted black olives
- 500g Yukon potatoes
- 180g *gorgonzola* cheese
- 30g walnuts, chopped roughly
- 2 shallots
- 100g bacon
- Whipped cream
- 300g raw prawns
- ½ tbsp of dry thyme leaves
- Zest of half a lemon
- 60g feta cheese
- ¼ tsp chilli flakes or powder
- 2 small fennel, washed and cut in fine slices of 5mm
- 100ml *pastis*
- 10g fresh tarragon
- 2 big *chicories* or 4 small ones
- 2 slices of cooked ham
- 50g grated *Gruyère* or *Comté* cheese
- A pinch of nutmeg

Basics from your pantry

- 370g flour
- 120cl of milk
- Butter
- 2 vegetable stock cubes
- 1 brown onion
- 3 garlic cloves
- 1 beef or vegetable bouillon cube
- 1 tsp tomato coulis
- 1 egg
- Olive oil
- Salt and pepper
- 250ml red wine
- ½ tsp dry oregano
- A pinch of paprika
- 300g rice

Breakfast: Green tea, fried eggs, baguette and bananas
Lunch: Salmon steak with *béchamel* sauce
and brown rice with fresh herbs
Dinner: *Polenta à la Niçoise*

BREAKFAST

Green tea
2 eggs
Butter
Vegetable oil

Baguette
Salt and pepper
2 bananas

Heat a knob of butter and a bit of oil in a pan. Crack and fry your eggs with salt and pepper. Let the yolk become a bit runny, and when ready, make some *tartine* with the butter and submerge them in the egg yolk.

NUTRITIONIST'S NOTE

Peppermint

The formidable effects of one of the most attractive herbs are countless; it can be used in a regulating tonic, relieving tired stomachs and livers, regulating flatulence and purifying the intestine. It is also a powerful help with digestion and helps to balance the overall digestive system.

A few mint leaves in a delicious, fresh salad or chewed at the end of a meal will make all the difference!

LUNCH

2 salmon steak
50g butter
50g flour
60cl of milk
200g brown rice
Parsley
Chives or tarragon or both

Olive oil
Salt and pepper
Half a lemon

Bring some water to the boil with two big pinches of salt. Prepare the *béchamel* sauce. In a pan, melt the butter. Then add the flour, whisk and add the milk all at once. Stir regularly, and you will feel that the sauce gets thicker at the bottom of your pan. Carry on stirring until the sauce has a custard consistency. Turn off the heat.

When the water is boiling and you put the rice in, start to cook the salmon. Heat a pan with the oil, grill the salmon on skin side first for four minutes on each side. Wash and chop your herbs finely. Reheat the *béchamel* sauce. Drain the rice and add the fresh herbs, mixing well. Place the rice and the salmon on the side in a nice plate. Add a good squeeze of lemon on the salmon and top with the *béchamel* sauce either on the salmon or rice or both.

NUTRITIONIST'S NOTE

Savoury

A pretty plant, typical of the South of France, it is at home in fields of thyme and lavender. In ancient times, it was always used in recipes for liqueurs, thanks to its digestive qualities.

Although it is no longer frequently used for pharmaceutical purposes, it is still very much enjoyed in everyday cooking due to its sharp, unmistakable fragrance.

It is also an ideal dish for lovers, as it boosts the libido.

DINNER

250g polenta
1 litre of water
1 vegetable cube bouillon
50g parmesan cheese
100g white mushrooms
Olive oil
1 handful of pitted black olives
For the tomato sauce (if you don't have any more in your freezer):
1 brown onion (on the list of basics)
2 garlic cloves (on the list of basics)
1 beef or vegetable bouillon cube

1 tsp tomato coulis
1 big can of tomato in juice
1 splash of red or white wine (optional)
Olive oil
Salt and pepper
Herbs de Provence

You should have prepared two lots of tomato sauce for Day Four and frozen it. If so, defrost it the day before by putting your container in the fridge first. Then in the day, leave it out of your fridge for a few hours if it's still frozen. Defrosting should be done in steps; first, put the food in the fridge so as not to radically change the temperature. It's bad to take a container out of the freezer and leave it out to defrost on the surface straight away. If you haven't frozen your tomato sauce, here is the recipe again: Peel and slice the onion. Peel and chop the garlic very finely. Brown them both in a pan with olive oil. When the onion is translucent, add the tomato *coulis*. Mix well and add the tomatoes in juice. Put the heat very low and let it simmer after adding salt and pepper. It needs to simmer for a few hours. The more it simmers, the better it will be.

When the liquid of the tomatoes disappears, add a bit of water and the bouillon cube. Taste and adjust the seasoning with *herbes de Provence* and salt and pepper. It will bubble a bit, and the idea is to add a bit of water at a time. When it gets brown and dry, add some more little by little. Stay around, mix and taste regularly. Add the splash of wine at the end and stop it after a few minutes to let the alcohol to evaporate.

While the tomato sauce is simmering (or defrosting) boil one litre of water with two good pinches of salt. Meanwhile, wash and slice your mushrooms, heat some olive oil in pan and fry them for five minutes on medium heat. When the water is boiling, plunge the polenta in at once and stir continuously for five minutes. (If not, it can spit and the polenta could form some lumps, which we don't want). The polenta grains will rise a bit and it will become thicker. The right consistency is the custard consistency, not too runny but still smooth. When the polenta is cooked, add a splash of good olive oil and stir. Place it on a serving plate. Add the tomato sauce on the top, then the mushrooms and olives and grate the parmesan on the top.

Breakfast: Black coffee, oat flakes, banana and honey
Lunch: *Gnocchi gorgonzola* and walnuts
Dinner: Eggs *meurette gratin*

BREAKFAST

Black coffee
2 tbsp of oats
1 tbsp of coconut flakes

Agave syrup or honey to your taste
Milk

Heat up the milk. When warm, turn off the heat and add the oats. Let it be on the side for a few minutes. Add the honey and coconut flakes and eat warm.

LUNCH

500g Yukon potatoes
1 egg yolk
250g flour
20g salt

180g *gorgonzola* cheese (available in all good Italian deli or organic shops)
30g shelled walnuts, chopped roughly
Salt and pepper

Gnocchi sound difficult to make but they're not. This is something you can definitely do very quickly. The thing that takes the longest is boiling the potatoes. This is the simplest and easiest way to make them, like my mum does. Please do not buy those 'ready to fry' or 'ready to cook' already-made *gnocchi*. They are tasteless and chewy ... really.

Boil one litre of water with two good pinches of salt. Peel and rinse the potatoes. Cut them into cubes of four or six (according to their size) and boil them until they are tender (for around 15 minutes). Mash them with a masher to obtain a very smooth purée. Add the egg yolk and mix. Add the salt, and little by little, add the flour, mixing well in between.

Once the purée is soft but hard enough to become a dough, form a bowl with your hands. Divide it in four with a knife. Flour your work place or table well and with each part of dough form some 'sausage', each of around 1cm diameter. Roll them with your hands, and once you have a few sausages, do the same with the other part of dough. If they stick to the workplace, sprinkle a bit of flour. Boil 500ml of water with two good pinches of salt.

While the water is heating, prepare your sauce by heating a pan, cut the *gorgonzola* into cubes of 1cm and put them in the pan on medium heat. The cheese will melt. When it's all melted, add the cream at once, then add some salt and pepper and stir gently. After five minutes and when the sauce is thicker, stop the heat and add the walnuts.

Plunge your *gnocchi* in the boiling water for two minutes. You'll see when they're ready – they will float up to the surface of the water. Drain them and put them on a nice plate and pour the sauce on the top. If you have too much sauce, don't waste it! You can freeze it! (See batch cooking section.)

DINNER

20g flour	50g mushrooms, washed and sliced
10g butter	Salt and pepper
2 shallots	250ml red wine
4 eggs	Whipped cream
100g bacon	

Melt the butter in a pan and then add the shallots, mushrooms and bacon. When the shallots are translucent, add three-quarters of the red wine. When it's bubbling, sprinkle in the flour to thicken your sauce.

Add salt and pepper. Taste and check the consistency. If it's too thick, add a bit of wine. If it's too liquid, add a bit of flour. In four ramekins or a baking dish, crack the eggs on the top of the shallots/wine/mushrooms mix. Add salt, pepper and put it in the oven for 15 minutes at 180°C until the egg yolks are cooked but still a bit runny.

NUTRITIONIST'S NOTE

Wild Garlic

Notable since at least the 7th century AD as one of the most beneficial herbs, wild garlic contains sulphur compounds which help detoxify the liver.

The advantage of this variety over classic garlic is that the garlicky taste is very much present but without the disadvantage of bad breath... rather more pleasant when sharing a meal with someone!

Breakfast: Black coffee, croissant or *pain au chocolat*
Lunch: *Hachis parmentier* (gratin of meat and mash potatoes), green salad
Dinner: *Endives au jambon* (chicory wrapped in ham)

BREAKFAST

Croissant or *pain au chocolat*

Black coffee

LUNCH

200g minced beef
150g potatoes mashed
1 onion
1 garlic clove
Half a tbsp of flour
50g tomato in juice
1 egg yolk
1 pinch of *herbes de Provence*
15g parmesan cheese

25g butter
25g *Gruyère* cheese or *Comté* (to grate)
Vegetable oil
A knob of butter
Rocket salad
Olive oil
Salt and pepper

Peel and chop the garlic and onion very finely. Heat a frying pan and melt a knob of butter and a splash of oil. Let them cook slowly on medium heat till they are soft. Add the tomato cut into cubes and then the beef, flour, salt and pepper, *herbes de Provence*. When the meat is cooked, stop the heat and add the yolk and the parmesan cheese and mix well.

Preheat the oven to 200°C.

Make your mashed potatoes. Peel and cut the potatoes into four or six (depending on their size). Boil 500ml of water with two good pinches of salt. Cook your potatoes for around 15 minutes (until tender). Mash them with a masher. Spread the meat mix in a baking tray for two, spread the mash potatoes on it, sprinkle with the grated cheese and put in the oven for 20 minutes. Meanwhile, prepare your salad and drizzle a bit of olive oil on your leaves.

DINNER

2 big chicories (or 4 small ones)
2 slices of cooked ham
50g butter and basics
50g flour
60cl of milk

50g *Gruyère* or *Comté* cheese (to grate)
Salt and pepper
A pinch of nutmeg

Bring 500ml of water to the boil with two big pinches of salt. Wash the chicories and take off the first leaves. Cut them in half lengthwise and remove the hard core with a knife. Plunge them in water and cook them for 10 minutes if they are small, 15 if they are big. Drain them and let them cool down a bit. The taste of your chicories will be even nicer if you pan fry them very slowly with butter and a bit of oil: we call that *braiser* in French.

Make your *béchamel* sauce:

In a pot, melt the butter. When it's melted, pour the flour and whisk. When it's all well mixed, pour the milk and whisk again.

Add salt and pepper and nutmeg. Stay around and whisk very often until you feel the sauce get thicker at the bottom of your pot. Stop the heat when your sauce has a custard consistency. Wrap your chicories in ham (cut in half according to the size of the chicories). Place them in a baking tray. Spread the béchamel sauce on top.

Preheat the oven to 180°C, grate the cheese on the top of your tray and bake for 15 minutes.

NUTRITIONIST'S NOTE

Edible plants which help to eliminate the effects of wine

If we could only save one herb, it would have to be desmodium. Very well known in the tropics in India, Africa and America, it acquired its mystical status in the west in the 1990s and early 2000s.

This major liver-protection herb decreases inflammation in the liver, powerfully regenerates hepatic cells and helps eliminate the effects of alcohol – among other benefits.

Now you know what you need to do to avoid nausea, headaches, bloating, heaviness and fatigue.

A hangover is the inevitable price paid for indulging in wine!

Desmodium can be put into vials, herbal teas and tablets... It really is an antidote to have in your 'natural pharmacy'.

MY FRENCH SECRETS

APPENDIX 1: BATCH COOKING

THIS IS the new and very useful trend for people who want to eat well without spending too much time in the kitchen.

On these lists of your seven-day dietary programme, you can double or triple the proportions of almost every dish. Nearly everything can be frozen. If you have a piece of cheese left (*Comté, Gruyère*, soft cheese like Camembert, blue cheese like Roquefort...), they go well in the freezer and will be great defrosted. Rice and pasta can be frozen too. You can make a portion, weigh it and put each in cling film like a well-wrapped little parcel and freeze your brown rice or pasta to defrost when needed. Cooked vegetables are good to go in the freezer too! (*Ratatouille*, cooked green beans, boiled potatoes...) all soups, gratins, beef bourguignon and tomato sauce, of course! Cooked fish like the salmon, the sauce for the egg *meurette* (mushrooms, shallots, wine...) can be frozen too!

You can prepare two lots of the prawns (as you will love them, I am sure), then freeze half of it and impress your friends when they come for dinner. The sauces are great to freeze, like the tomato sauce.

Asparagus, salad and fresh herbs really have to be fresh. I would not think twice about doubling the size of your portion and freeze!

APPENDIX 2:
FOOD AND WINE PAIRING

F OOD AND wine pairing is such a vexed subject nowadays. Even a beginner starts their journey into wine asking their wine merchants to recommend food pairing. It's become such an important matter now that no one would believe that is very new to wine. Until the end of the 19th century, wine was only a drink, even (with beer) the *only* healthy drink to permit good hydration and avoid the usually toxic water that could bring illness.

Food and wine pairing history started at the end of the 19th century in Paris, when in the restaurants consumers wanted to get the same experience they had had back in Lyon. Beaujolais wines were then viewed as the best way to enjoy food. But still, we were not yet being picky in term of perfect match.

There is no Tinder app for food and wine pairing, and actually the first rule is: *Forget about the rules!*

Taste is personal, but if you are looking for a better experience, here are my tips. Those tips are coming from more than 10 years of Food & Wine pairing education as part of the WSET global education, but also more than 40 years of food experiment being grown in a very epicurean family. (I could add that my personal sensitivity makes me very picky when it comes to food and wine.)

The first questions you need to ask yourself are:
- Are you (or your guests) a coffee ristretto drinker, or a cappuccino drinker...thus, do you like bitterness, or do you have a sweet tooth?
- When it comes to water, are you still team or sparkling team? Thus, do you enjoy acidity!

Coffee and sparkling water drinkers are usually good clients for a glass of wine.

Now when it comes to food pairing, it's actually very important to understand that what will play a major role is more the flavours (acidity, sourness, bitterness, saltiness, umami) than the aromas. I can see your surprise here. Sommeliers since the 1960s have been telling everyone how and why the "strawberry aromas" of the Beaujolais makes it a perfect match on a strawberry pie. Or the "cocoa flavours" of a Maury make it perfect with a chocolate cake. I would say no... And no...

The aromas are the same, but it matches because the structure of the wine allowed those pairing. Let me explain... or better, let's do an experiment.

Take a glass of your favourite wine (really do it...don't worry, we are not starting without you). Take a sip of it, and try to be aware about how fast you are salivating just after. Take another sip, and if it's red, try again to be aware about how the wine (the tannin part) is drying out your gums, tongue, etc... Make a memory of the flavour intensity.

You've just drunk in mindfulness. Congratulations!

Now, go for a walk and buy some organic lemon, some salt and some sweet biscuits. Redo the first exercise, but take a second step with a hint of lemon (acidity) before drinking. Pause, take a moment to analyse. Does it make your wine more acidic? No. You will be surprised to find out that your wine seems less acidic, fruitier, rounder, richer.

Do the same with salt... It works with all type of wines, as the salt will combine with the tannins to soften them. Magic!

However, if you do the same with sugar, that will be another story... Sweetness is not very friendly to wine. It makes it feel drier, less fruity, astringent and so on...

Enough, with exercise, let's go into practical tips!

What food should I have with...WHITE WINES?

With the exception of Gewürztraminer, Viognier, Muscat, the main feature of many white wines is ACIDITY. When you think white wine, you might think crisp, fresh, easy drinking, aperitif... the question is then: what about sweetness? Here are my recommendation depending on the sweetness of your white.

Light Dry white wine
(Pinot Grigio, Sancerre, Chablis, New Zealand Sauvignon Blanc, Chardonnay Limari Valley Chile, Chenin Blanc, Riesling, etc.)

Those wines are said to be light and crispy, and could be neutral in aroma (Chablis) to aromatic (Sauvignon Blanc, Riesling).

Think "fat"! Fat food tends to decrease the acidity sensation, so from your fave, fish and chips or salt and pepper squid to your best cheese board, these wines are low risk. Say, savoury cake or Feta cheese. But also, for those salty and fresh Greek salads or seafood.

Dry Riesling aromatic is well known to pair well with Thai and Vietnamese food as it enhances lemongrass and coriander.

On the veggie side, think falafel, courgettes, veggie tempura.

Full-bodied Dry White Wine
(White Burgundy, Australian and Californian Chardonnay, Chenin Blanc from South Africa or the Loire Valley)

Here is the wine that is considered sometimes as "fat". Those wines are usually (but not always) matured in oak barrels, or on the "lees" (i.e. yeast that stays inside the wine), or has been made using other fermentation techniques. However, they all have this in common: that it adds to the classic aromatic wine a rich texture with aromas like vanilla, coconut, butter, brioche... Those wines are less easy to drink on their own and deserve a more complex dish than the light dry white wines.

Think poultry in creamy sauce, or all kind of mushroomy dishes with cream. Veal sweetbreads with Morilles are a classic with a Meursault white. But you don't have to be very exotic, as your Sunday roast will do too. Blanquette de veau for a traditional option. Spaghetti carbonara, polenta...

On the veggie side, think halloumi, or Indian or Thai curry: vegetable tikka masala, daal. You got it?

Creamy cheese also, as Brillat Savarin, Chaource, Buffalo Mozzarella.

On the Pizza side, go for the Bianca – the very cheesy ones.

Off Dry White or Rosé wine (still and sparkling)
(Southwest of France, Côtes de Gascogne, German Riesling, White Zinfandel, Lambrusco, Moscato d'Asti)

There are fewer food-pairing options in this category. This is a classic option for a glass of wine in a restaurant. Very often, this is an aperitif companion, as those wines tend to lack intensity of flavour: antipasti with tomatoes, artichokes, feta cheese... Thus, they are not the best to pair with a classic dish, as the wine's taste would be overwhelmed. Stay on the fresh side; say, Greek salad or falafel, as for the light white wines.

Don't miss them with light desserts, such as fruit salad, Pavlova, or clementine or apricot pie. One of my favourite: roasted peaches from the Piedmont with a Muscat d'Asti!

What food should I have with...RED WINES?

Light Red Wine
(Red Burgundy, Sonoma or Chilean Pinot noir, Beaujolais, Barbera, Dolcetto)

Those easy-drinking wines are the best seller. Due to their light structure, they can be enjoyed by the glass. If you wish to have them with some food, be aware that only the aroma will play an important part. Pinot Noir or Gamay are quite aromatic, so they can pair with intense meals that have simpler structures, such a little game meat (pheasant, hare, partridge, giblets...) or wild mushrooms but also many kind of fish.

Those wines are low-risk. They match with cheeses, tomato sauce based meal. One of my favourite pairings is a Dolcetto d'Alba with cuttlefish in ink with polenta. From the recipes in this book, you could try brown bread tartine with mushrooms (page 106) or *croque monsieur* with Parma ham (page 99).

Medium bodied and aromatic wines
(Syrah based wines: Rhône, Australia, California, Chile)

"La Syrah" is a feminine grape from the Rhône valley. I will focus on her strong personality. This is *the* grape that can produce the greatest wine in the world on its own (Hermitage AOC in France) but can also be a great blend.

There are berry aromas with a wild range of components, from pepper to blackberry jam but also violet, plum, liquorice, leather and so on.

Syrah has its lovers and its haters. But if you are a lover, know that its structure expresses on the tongue and not on your gums, which make it easily palatable and even more loveable.

These wines give you the sensation that they are quite soft (but they are not) with plenty of aroma. That's the reason why they deserve a special place in this book, as they are almost the only ones made to match with lamb or spicy food from South America and North Africa. Be careful with the alcohol, but if you are a lover of wines with character, those pairings are very much for you. In this book, go for the Spanish tortilla (page 81), grilled chorizo and red pepper salad (page 81), rosemary lamb cutlets (page 108). Clafoutis, cherry tomato, black olives and thyme (page 69), as well as black olive tapenade, are exquisite with Syrah-based wines.

Full body red wines
(Bordeaux communal wines, Malbec, Chianti, Barolo, Napa Valley, Douro and Dão wines, Ribera del Duero, Rioja...)

Those very structured and complex wines need complex dishes with proteins...not necessarily just animal protein (think Lasagna al forno, for example).

The best recipes here are mushroom omelette (page 101) with a Bordeaux or Chianti wine. Sirloin steak à l'échalotte (page 103) with an Argentinian Malbec or a Rioja Reserva.

How does it work? Proteins tend to soften the tannins, as for the salt. Try it, grab your favourite deep intense red and have a sip on its own. Then take some pure salt and sip again...

You got it?

That's the reason why, in South West of France, foie gras is served with some *fleur de sel* instead of chutney, to be able to match the South West red wine structure. For chutney, rendezvous with the sweet wines instead.

What food should I have with...CHAMPAGNE?
(Or other traditional methods, from Cava to Cap Classique, or Franciacorta.)

From the lightest expression to the most complex wine, Champagne is not a unique style and so can fit plenty of different dishes. The lees ageing give it a complex expression. For me, it's the best companion for a cheese board, no matter how complex it is.

For the best expression, you can follow the same rules than for Burgundy wines, either red or white. But have you thought about pairing those splendid wines with something more simple? Finger foods, tapas, salads... Just try it! You don't have to wait for big occasion to open a bottle of traditional sparkling wine: opening the bottle is the occasion! By the glass, for aperitif, with a main dish...

My only recommendation would be to forget it with the dessert. Sweetness so increases the sensation of acidity that it transforms the champagne into something tasteless and tart. Still, if you want to do it with dessert, select an extra-dry or semi-sweet version of sparkling wine.

The perfect matches from the recipes in this book will be pea soup & Parmesan cheese (page 58), spring courgette gratin (page 61), pumpkin soup (page 100), lentil salad (page 104)...

MY FRENCH SECRETS

What food should I have with...SWEET WINES?
(German Riesling, Eiswein, BA and TBA, Vendanges Tardives and SGN Alsace, Canadian Ice wine, Tokaji, Sauternes...)

Somehow those wines seem to be out of fashion, perhaps thanks to their calories, which used to be their main advantage in old times but now is seen as a warning! However, served in moderation, these styles of wine might be the food's best friend.

They have a great aromatic intensity and can last for a long time when opened in your fridge, so you don't have to finish the bottle in one go...

Coming back to our foie gras with chutney, this is where you will serve a Vendange Tardive, Pinot Gris or Gewürztraminer.

Sweet and sweet don't make more sweetness in your mouth; this is quite the opposite. Sweetness in your plate balances the sweetness in your wine (but not in your blood!). Choose lightly sweet wines with your light dessert (fresh fruits, pavlova, etc.).

Find out how Asian food (Thai, Japanese) goes well with those wines. Try the following:

- Sweet potato, grilled chickpeas with lemon and tahini sauce (page 97) with Alsace Riesling or Vendange Tardive.
- Salmon and green apple tartare (page 64) with German Riesling Spätlese.
- Prawns with fennel, pastis sauce and rice (page 72) with a Moscato d'Asti.
- A plate of fraîcheur burrata, watermelon, melon, etc. with a semi-sweet white Côte de Gascogne.
- Rocket salad with fresh apricot, roasted hazelnuts, feta, etc. with Sauternes.

Then think cheese. These wines are easier to pair with cheese than red, as they don't have any conflicted tannins:

- Cheese board, Stilton with Port, Roquefort with Sauternes
- Hot goat cheese salad with a Côteaux du Layon.

Be curious. Try some new wines. Have Champagne and find your best pairing, the one you love. Think about your pleasure first, and never forget that the best food and wine pairing is "the one you favour"...

GOODBYE NOTE FROM THE AUTHOR

THIS BOOK has been a long-matured process, and I really hope you enjoy the ride as much as I did. Like we say, it's not the destination but the journey that is the most enjoyable.

I hope this book helps you to enjoy life while staying slim and healthy and gives you a lot of ideas and the desire to cook new things, to be bold and curious and to explore everything that food has to give us.

While cooking every day at my restaurant and waiting to start a second book, I wish you all the cooking and happiness in the world!

With love, Marlène xxx